Over $250 in
Free Bonuses
Over $3,499 in Educational Grants & Credits

FREE FREE FREE FREE

fast track

TO eBaY

An Introduction to Profiting with Online Auctions

Larry Yakiwczuk

www.FastTrackToEbay.com

Fast Track to eBay:
An Introduction to Profiing with Online Auctions

Copyright ©2016

Contents

Introduction

You would think this book is about eBay but it's more than that. We use eBay as a reference to what you can do on any internet auction site. Even though we talk about eBay and eBay auctions, what we are really talking about is internet sales in general and specifically Internet auctions. Most internet auction sites operate in the same manner that eBay does. You list your items for sale, people bid on them driving the price up, and then at some point the item sells and you get paid for the product. Also most internet auction sites have some form of feedback system, some sort of email system and some sort of payment system built into them. We will touch on and discuss all these things here.

In this book we will talk about various ideas and various ways to do different things that relate to Internet auctions. In particular we specifically talked about sourcing products. That means how do you find products to sell and where do you find them and how do you get them. We will also talk about one of the best ways to make money through internet auctions and that is consignment selling. Consignment selling is where you don't actually own the products that you sell. People who have product to sell will consign the product with you, you sell the product, you collect the payment, and then you give the owner of the products a percentage of the money that you have received. I consider consignment selling probably the single best way to make money with Internet auctions.

I will also talk about packaging items and how to safely package them for shipping to various parts of the country. You will find out what sort of packaging materials to use and where to get them for the cheapest amount of money, or even for free. We will also talk about different ways of shipping items, what is the best way to ship an item, whether to use a postal service, courier service or some kind of special delivery service.

Some of the more advanced things we will talk about is how to specifically deal with competitors. You're not the only one that's going to be selling or using internet auctions. How do you deal with people that are trying to take business away from you and how do you take business away from them. Also there are a lot of scams out there on the Internet and in particular a lot of internet auction scams. We will show you how to spot the scams, how to avoid them, and if you do get caught, some various methods that you can try to recover and recoup the money you've lost.

Finally we'll talk on the subject that is the most important thing when it comes to Internet auctions and internet sales or anything that you do in the real world. And that is taking action. Learning and educating yourself is all good and fine but you will never get anything done unless you actually take some action. Taking that first step can sometimes be very scary. However it's something that you have to do. A lot of times it really doesn't matter whether you make a mistake doing something or whether you do it right, the important thing is that you do something and it really doesn't matter what you do, as long as you do it.

As you are aware from the front cover there are free bonuses included with this book. To get your FREE bonuses all you have to do is go to our website:

www.FastTrackToEbay.com/book

These Bonuses are in addition to the FREE Bonuses listed on the public website. After you input your name and contact information you'll be given access to your FREE bonuses.

Among these bonuses is a fee credit on a major internet auction site. Just by registering an ID on this auction site, we will give you a fee credit of approximately twice the value of this book. This credit can be used for any listing upgrades on the site or even for advertising on the site. Some of the other bonuses you'll receive will be mp3 audio files of some various interviews that I have done over the recent past.

If after reading this book, you decide that selling on the internet through Internet auctions is for you, and you want to make a living doing it, we can help you with that. Besides this book we also have published a complete educational course package of buying and selling using internet auctions. If you are seriously interested in learning more, please check in the bonus section as we can give you very big discounts off the retail price of what these courses normally sell for, through our Educational Grant program. This is an added bonus because you took action and got this book. We also have another added bonus for you if you purchase these discounted courses. Any amount you pay for any of our advanced educational materials or any products we have for sale, we will give you that equivalent amount as a fee credit on a major internet auction site. See the bonuses section for full details.

My hope is that this book will give you an insight into what is possible and how much you can actually make if you put your mind to it. Remember if you treat this like a hobby it will pay like a hobby, if you treat it like a business it will pay like a business. Many people have used eBay and Internet auctions to generate a full time income for themselves while only working part time. My hope is that you can do this as well. So what I am Telling You is to just read this book, take some action, be a success, and then let me know how well you have done.

1   Introduction and background of EBay

EBay started back in 1995 when Pierre Omidyar made up a website to sell his broken laser pointer. Then by 1997 the EBay site had sold over 1 million items. Now EBay is the world's largest online shopping marketplace. **In 2005 EBay sold a gross merchandise volume of 45 Billion dollars**. EBay Operates worldwide in over 33 different countries, with over 200 million registered users. At any particular time EBay has approximately 100 million items available for sale with over 6.5 million items added each day. It is estimated that a digital camera is sold every minute and a musical instrument is sold every 30 seconds. The most expensive item ever sold has been a Gulfstream Jet which went for 4.9 million dollars.

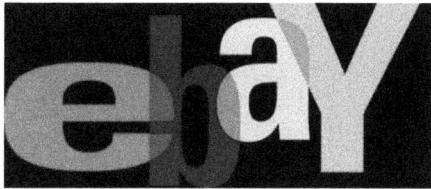

Often I get asked why I started an EBay business and why I think it is the perfect home based business. Personally I believe that everyone should be buying and selling on EBay. It is the perfect business because you can do it from home and set your own hours. You can work as little or as much as you want. You can start selling items with very little time commitment, and you can do the computer work and email at your own pace. Personally I do email in the evenings during commercials while I am watching TV.

You don't need any special skills to sell on EBay; all you need is basic computer knowledge and be able to figure out how to use a digital camera. If you do have some kind of specialized knowledge that is even better as you can use that information to specialize your sales to specific markets. There is also no need to carry a large inventory. In fact when someone is just starting out, I recommend that they sell merchandise that they already have. The average person has between $1500 and $2000 worth of stuff sitting in their basement gathering dust. They could sell this stuff and never even miss it. Think of that ugly old Thing-a-ma-jig you got from your great aunt 2 years ago, which has been gathering dust in the closet. You have always been afraid to re-gift it because everyone knows she gave it to you. Well now you can sell it on EBay and ship it across the country without her ever finding out that you got rid of it. **Another big advantage about EBay is that there is no big outlays of cash at start up**. There is no special equipment needed, you don't have to rent store space, and you don't need employees.

Another big advantage is that you can get the whole family involved and turn some of your hobbies into a working business. Now when you go to a garage sale with your

spouse, you can buy items to sell on EBay rather than just fill up your garage with them. Also you can get the kids involved; they can clean and package items, and carry packages to the post office for you. When the kids grow out of their cloths or get tiered of their new toys, you can just sell them on EBay rather than throw them out. Also you can buy their replacements on EBay as well. Now you are not only generating cash but saving money as well! If you have hobbies then you can use your specialized knowledge to increase your own collections or deal in that type of merchandise with authority. The thing I like best about selling on EBay, is that **I do not have to deal with customers directly in a face-to-face manner**. Everything is done through email and I never have to speak to a single customer.

The most important advantage about an EBay business is that you are the master of your own destiny. The more items you sell, the more income you generate. **Remember if you treat you're selling like a hobby then it will pay you like a hobby, BUT if you treat it like a business then it will pay you like a business**. Also because it is a home based business, you will get numerous tax advantages such as deductions for a home office and mileage on your vehicle while looking for sale items.

1.1 Making EBay a Business

Making the occasional sale on EBay doesn't require any particular long-range planning or structure to your activities. Each sale is an activity in itself; it starts when you decide you want to sell the item, lasts for as long as you've still got it, and then ends when the customer has the item and you've got your payment.

If you're going to be selling on a larger scale, however, it will quickly become inefficient and confusing to treat each sale in isolation. You'll want to create an organized system for handling inventory, sales, and money – in short, a business. A business doesn't necessarily have to be a full-time endeavor, it can still remain just a hobby or past time, but it provides structure that will help you keep track of everything you need to keep track of.

Your EBay business will start out small, but it is a business nonetheless and there are many principles that are common to all businesses. If you're conducting your business as a hobby you may not need to adhere closely to all of them, but in general it's good to at least know what to expect.

Firstly, given the vastness and diversity of the online business world, in all probability **you're not alone in whatever it is you're doing**. There will be competitors out there who are buying and selling the same sorts of things you are. It's important to keep an eye on your competition; they can take business away from you and you can take business away from them. They may have ideas you can use for yourself, and they may have made mistakes that you can take advantage of to draw more customers for yourself.

Secondly, **it costs money to make money**. Running a business will entail a variety of expenses. Even if you've got no employees and are running your business out of your home, there are still many little fees and costs for supplies that will add up to a significant sum. Be prepared to spend money up front for things that will prove useful over the long run

Finally, the goal is profits but you'll sometimes take losses. Losses are a routine part of business and shouldn't spook you too badly. Take risks and accept the occasional loss as just another cost of doing business. That's not to say that one shouldn't pay attention to losses or keep track of them; if you continue to take losses in the long run then there's likely something more than just bad luck at work. You may need to reconsider your way of doing business or even your overall business plan if it turns out that you can't make a net profit doing what you're currently doing. Be prepared to change your mind.

1. **Create a business-only email address** – this both helps you keep track of customer correspondence more easily and keeps it from intruding on your personal life when you want to be "off the clock". Also you will need a separate bank account – A separate repository for your EBay earnings can make it much easier to keep track of them. Also, your bank may offer business-related services that will be of use, such as foreign currency balances. And finally you will need a separate credit card – Similarly, this will help you keep track of business expenses more easily, as well as preventing personal credit issues from intruding on your business' operation.

2. If you're operating your business out of your home, you will probably also want to **create a business-only space within your home** (a home office) in order to help segregate your business and personal life. If possible you could even keep to a consistent schedule for working on your EBay business, segregating your business and personal time.

3. In addition to various registrations to be made online, there are other legal issues to address when setting up a small business. You should visit your local license and registration office to find out more. Things you may need to do include: 1) Applying for a business license, 2) Filing for a GST Number (needed for sales tax), and 3) Registering your copyrights, trademarks, and patents. For most businesses this will simply mean registering the business' name and logo as trademarks.

You likely won't need to do all of these things right away, since it's perfectly legal for private citizens to buy and sell items in an impromptu manner within reasonable limits. You may wish to "test the waters" by getting started on EBay before you've completed all of this paperwork. However, don't put it off for long. Having a properly licensed and registered business opens up many advantageous tax opportunities, such as writing off business-related expenses.

1.2   Why EBay is a great business in a recession

Some people say the recession we are currently in, is a bad thing. I hear this everywhere I go, and at times I cannot keep myself from laughing out loud (lol for you texters). For people who know how things work and how to sell on EBay, **this so called recession is one of the best things to happen in recent times**. Just another example of how contrarian thinking is probably the best way to look at things. Selling on EBay is one of the best hedges against the recession, there is. Whenever the economy is down, people really start to conserve their money and look hard for bargains. The result of this is that everyone heads for the internet and directly to EBay where they think they can get some real bargains. And this is where all of us power sellers are willing to help them by relieving them of their cash. Whenever the economy is down, EBay sales are up.

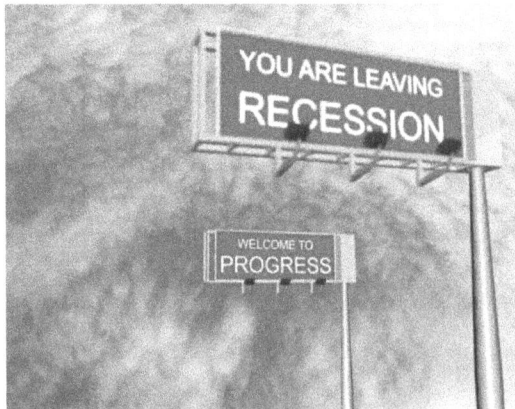

Another benefit of a slow or declining economy is that there are a lot more business failures and bankruptcies. This provides for lots of distressed merchandise sales and auctions where we can pick up good salable merchandise for literally pennies on the dollar. Check your local newspapers and I am pretty sure you will see at least a couple of bankruptcy auctions every month, regardless of what city you live in. Currently I do not attend many auctions as a purchaser anymore, but after talking to some of my local auctioneer friends I may have to rethink that. They told me that they cannot believe how things have changed over the last six months. They are so busy trying to liquidate the excess merchandise that they are actually turning down consignments. One auctioneer I know is actually backlogged over 4 months on merchandise to sell. That means he could stop taking in new consignments and still sell for four months before running out of stuff. Also they told me that the buying public has not really started turning to auction sales yet, to buy their stuff. So now is the perfect sweet spot in the cycle, lots of merchandise to purchase, with very little competition for it. This results in dirt-cheap prices.

As everyone knows and has heard, the current economy also has had a major effect on the real estate market. The resulting drop in value has resulted in a growing number of foreclosures. Many of these foreclosures result in a large number of those people actually abandoning many of their possessions in the foreclosed property. The institutions or people foreclosing have to dispose of those things in some manner. Most people just call in the disposal bins and fill them up with stuff and then send them to the auction houses for disposal. However as I mentioned previously the auction companies are getting so busy that they are now refusing to accept a lot of these consignments, so these bins are now just headed to the dump. Wouldn't it be nice if somebody contacted their local bank or foreclosure company and struck a deal with them to take this excess merchandise off their hands?

Landlords also have a similar problem when tenants either skip out on their rent or are evicted. As an active landlord I cannot tell you how many times I have had to clean out an apartment and not known what to do with all the stuff that was left behind (of course that was before I learned how to sell on EBay). You would be totally amazed at what people would leave behind simply because it's not worth their time or energy to deal with their own stuff. I have found Cd's, DVD's, stereos, various personal collections (coins, stamps, etc.), and all kinds of consumer electronics. That's why even if you are only into real estate rentals; you should still get some education on how to sell on EBay. It's a good way to recover some of those lost rental dollars because of a bad tenant.

Car repossessions are also up because of the economy. Normally the repo companies just send the vehicles to local auctions for liquidations. But that generally does not get them top dollar for the sales. This is an opportunity for a clever EBay seller to jump in and cut a deal where they could market the repo'ed car on EBay for a percentage of the

final sale price.

1.3 Cutting through red tape (don`t cut corners!)

n this section, we are going to be talking about all the red tape you have to cut through when you expand your existing EBay business. In the past I have talked a little bit about the legal requirements and red tape that you have to go through when you first start up your EBay business. You first have to decide if you want to do business as a Corporation (Corp) or as a sole proprietorship (SP). If using an SP you are just operating under your own name, or you may want to register a trade name (TN) for your business. Registering a TN is fairly easy and only requires filling out and registering a few documents at the corporate registry and paying the fees. If using a CORP you need to incorporate and that will cost a few hundred dollars. If you want a corporate name instead of a number you will also have to do a name search which is an added expense, and you may not be able to use the name. If you just have a numbered CORP then you also get a TN by registering and paying. The next step is to get a bank account. As a SP it is fairly easy as it is just another personal bank account. If you have a TN then its a little more work as you will need to provide those documents to the bank as well. If you are a CORP, then you will have to give the bank all your incorporation documents as well as your personal information. Then if you have a TN for your CORP you will also have to give them those registration documents as well. Most banks also make you sign a pile of bank documents and corporate resolutions that give you the right to open the accounts. Some banks may require you to have a GST number before they will open your bank account. So next you will have to contact the government and fill out the paperwork application in order to get a GST number.

Now that you have a bank account and GST number, you need to check your local municipality for any special rules and regulations regarding your business operations. Most places require that you at least get a business license. So there is more paper work to fill out and wait for an answer. If operating out of your home, you will need a home based business license which may be easy or difficult. If you are just doing online sales and don't have customers coming to your house all you need is a minor development permit and then the business license. If you have people coming by, then you may need a major development permit before they will license you. A major permit may require a lot of paper work and time to get as the municipality may have to advertise your permit application and wait to see if any neighbors complain. Of course every step has application fees to deal with. Now if you are operating out of some other building besides your home, the process is even more complicated as zoning issues may come into play at that location. Most cities have specific zoning requirements for specific businesses. If your location is not zoned for your business type, you may have to apply for a zoning change or variance. Again more fees and time

wasted, and no guarantees that you will get the outcome you wanted. Also in a commercial location you may have to get fire and safety inspections before they will give you the business license. Again more time and fees. Are you starting to get a sense of how municipalities create all this red tape simply as a revenue generating system for themselves?

Assuming that you get to this point you are probably ready to open your doors and start doing business for the first time. Please do not underestimate the time that this whole process can take. It can be very speedy and only take a few weeks. Or it can be very lengthy and take many months or longer. Last year the process took my partner Jon over 9 months before he was actually able to open up his Crap-2-Cash consignment store front. The process may be lengthy, but it is vitally important that you follow the correct procedures and applications. If you don't, then all it will take is one person to make one complaint and you may be shut down, and or face numerous fines. It's tempting to cut corners, but don't do it.

1.4 Fast track to getting started: education & internships

A great way to get education is to volunteer and do an internship with someone already doing it. Successful EBay sellers will gladly share their time and knowledge with anyone willing to learn and spend time helping them out. As Darren Weeks (founder of Fast Track) always says be willing to work for free to get the experience and education. I personally know a number of Buckaru certified EBay sellers in the Edmonton area who would gladly take on an intern to help them learn how to sell and build their EBay business. It can be a lot of work, but trust me, it is definitely worth it. I wish there were people like that around when I started selling.

From my experience, **the best way to get experience in any field is to volunteer and work for free alongside someone who is already in the field you are interested in**. This is truly the fast track to success. You accelerate the steep learning curve learn about all the pitfalls without having to endure them yourself. Well I am happy to say that a young man named Mat from down east took me up on my challenge. He is already running a successful business but wanted to learn about EBay and consignment selling. He has taken time off from his own business and has come out west and volunteered to work with myself and my partner Jon Stachyruk at Jon's store called Crap-2-Cash. He has come out on his own dime and taking care of his own expenses. He is putting

in a lot of long days, seven days a week. He is motivated to learn anything he can. After a month or six weeks, when he is done here, he will be returning home and will be starting his own new business based on what he has leaned here. I have no doubt that he will actually be more successful back home than we are here. By doing research here in our market he has also realized that his home market (where he plans on setting up) is virgin territory and no one there has a consignment or second hand business running.

Motivation is a funny thing, and if you can find workers that are properly motivated you cannot help but to succeed. We have the case in point here with Mat. Jon currently employs two other people to work for him. For them it is just a job and there only motivation is to get a paycheck and the end of the pay period. There work is average at best. Mat on the other hand is motivated to work in order to learn. I can safely say that the amount of work he does is equivalent to both the other two employees put together, and he is not even getting paid. Motivation makes the difference. There are also a lot of books and course materials out there about selling on EBay. But before you go out and buy one of these packages, it is important that you do some due diligence first. When looking to purchase an EBay course package, the most important aspect to consider is whether or not you are going to get an education or are you just going to be paying an ongoing fee with no real support provided. Generally a good educational package will give you a complete and well-rounded Education. What I mean by that, is that it will address all aspects of starting an EBay business, even if you know nothing about EBay and are starting from square one. It should include Basics about EBay and how to properly set up your EBay accounts. It should also give you information about safe buying practices and how to protect yourself if you are a purchaser. Currently about 95% of people using EBay only use it for purchasing items for their own use. So even if you never sell an item on EBay you will still learn how to buy properly. This is also very important from a seller's perspective, in that you need to know the buyers concerns and how to address them properly. A good course should also cover both basic and advanced selling techniques. It should then move on to cover power selling and then explain how to turn your hobby into a thriving Internet business.

Selling is only a small part of an EBay business, so a good course will also cover some of the other aspects you need to know about, such as how to take good item photos and how to write good item descriptions and titles. Other important areas that need to be covered are how to properly package and ship an item. Choosing the proper shipping service could make or break your business, so that better be covered in the course. Another very important topic that MUST be covered is the area of product sourcing. For those of you not familiar with this term, all it means is how to find items to sell. I consider this single topic to be one of the single most important aspects of a profitable EBay business.

Another important aspect of a good course is that it presents realistic goals and expectations. If a course promoter tells you that you are going to get rich within 7 days, I would be a bit skeptical. But if they tell you that you will probably pay for the course in a few months, then that is a little more realistic. Don't get me wrong here, you can make really big profits really quickly, if you put your mind to it and do things properly, but don't count on it happening right off the start. Another important consideration to look at is whom the course is meant for. Is the course appropriate for Canadians or is it specifically written for the US market and are we just an additional cash cow for the US marketer? I consider this a very important point as most of the current books and course packages are written and produced for the American market and as such have little or no Canadian content. Trust me, selling from Canada is very different than selling from the US, and a good course will address those differences.

Now for some of the warning signs. Firstly, are you paying a fixed specified price for the course up front only, or are you being asked to subscribe to a recurring fee structure. I believe a good introductory course should be at a reasonable fixed price without any recurring fees for additional services. Also is the course actually teaching you how to sell items or teaching you to use some 3rd party software to make auction listings that sell items from drop shippers? In my opinion a course that promotes drop shipping, as your major selling practice should be very suspect. Remember if it sounds too good to be true, it probably is.

1.5 Networking

In this section I want to talk a little bit about networking and a few things I have noticed about different networking types of events. Then at the end of this section I will tell you about the best and most expensive event I have ever been at.

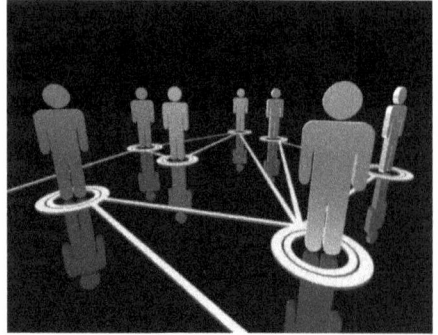

In my opinion the bottom end of the networking events are those that are put on by local groups and publicized as networking events. They generally restrict membership to one person in each type of business and run weekly meetings for their members. People at these events are only concerned about marketing their own business to the detriment of everyone else at the event. Generally no one is interested in what you have to say but more interested in telling you what they do and why you need their service.

The next type of networking events are actually not networking events, they are generally informational presentations for something. These are generally the types of events put on by Fast Track and other organizations. They are meant to be an educational event designed to inform the general public about some sort of product or service, or just for pure education. Everyone there is for the specific reason to learn something new. These are great events for networking as long as you do not overdo it. The important thing at these events is to talk to people and ask them what they do. If you show a sincere interest in other people's businesses they will naturally get around to asking you about yours. Be careful here, because if you are not interested in their business don't fain interest because it will be immediately obvious and all you will do is make the other person angry. Personally I always like to hear what other people are doing and are up to, because you never know when you might hear something new and exciting that may interest you. I have done very well at these events and have generated numerous investors.

The next type of event is the business or professional organization event. They are things like Rotary, University Alumni, and professional groups. These events are great places to meet other successful professionals usually in your own field. It's a great place to set up joint venture deals or find new investors. I always attend these types of events when I find out about them. They usually also have great free food there.

The Final type of event is something I had never really done before, but after doing this recent event I am hooked and sold on them. These events are the high profile, high cost, charity events that have nothing to do with business or networking as such. These are purely social events that people go to in order to help a good cause and have a ton of fun at the same time. They are generally very high priced for the VIP entrance but also have general public access as well. To the people that attend these events paying up to $5000 per person is nothing. And trust me when I say these are the type of people you want to be investing with you. Being able to spend time and have fun with these people is fantastic. Then when you actually start talking about business (which always happens at these events because all these people are successful business people) they listen to you and take you seriously because you have to be successful just to be there. This is the easiest way to buy respect and give the impression of success.

Now I will let you know about the event I attended. As a lot of you know I am ga-ga over exotic autos. The event I attended was an event called Race-the-Base and was a fund raising event for the military families' charities in Cold Lake Alberta. It was basically an event to let people race their cars on the 2.5 mile runways at the airbase, and it was billed as the only legal way to break 300 km/hr in your car. There were a total of about 60 vehicles and drivers as well as about 200 VIP's in attendance for this 3 day event. It was also open to the public as spectators. There was a special driver and VIP area and special private social events. It was a car watchers paradise; there were Ferrari's, Lamborghinis, Porsches, Jaguar's, Ford GT's, and others. I could not believe how successful some of these people were. One chap from BC was a venture cap person and he had 3 Lambo's, another person from Calgary brought 2 of his Ferraris. Generally everyone there was a very successful business owner of some sort, and there were no corporate suit types anywhere. You bond very quickly with people when you are talking about accelerating up to 300 km/hr in $250,000 dollar or more automobiles. I made some very good new friends at this event. Also every participant and their sponsors were immortalized in the event guide with their pictures and corporate advertising. This event guide was given to all drivers and VIP's at the event and was sold to the general public. This long lasting advertising will be held for a long time by anyone lucky enough to get one.

Also because I was a minor sponsor for this event I was able to give some VIP tickets to some business friends I know. They said it was the best event they were ever at, and they made many new business contacts that are going to be very profitable in the future. This was the best marketing and promotion money I have ever spent and it specifically targeted the ultra-successful entrepreneurs', and it was a hell of a lot of fun.

To check out this event you can go to www.racethebase.com for photos and info. To see in car video of my 282 km/hr run, check out my personal website at www.yakiwczuk.com.

1.6 Finding deep discounts when sourcing product

Recently I talked with my contact at a major educational institution who surpluses all their equipment. He told me that they have stopped sending their equipment to the local auctions because they were not getting any decent prices for the equipment.

Many years ago, this educational institution used to run their own auctions in order to surplus their excess equipment. They used to have a separate warehouse just for this endeavor. All the different departments would ship their excess equipment to this warehouse and they would generally fill up the warehouse and run an auction every 3-4 months. These were the absolute best auctions ever, and these were the very first auctions that I ever went to. They were the auctions that hooked me into the surplus merchandise market. I still remember my very first auction purchase. It was a multi I/O port board for a personal computer that allowed you to add 16 ports to the computer, where you could add on modems for a bulletin board system (BBS). Yes I used to run a small BBS system. I got this board for about $25, and I was ecstatic because I was just looking for a new one and they were retailing for over $500.

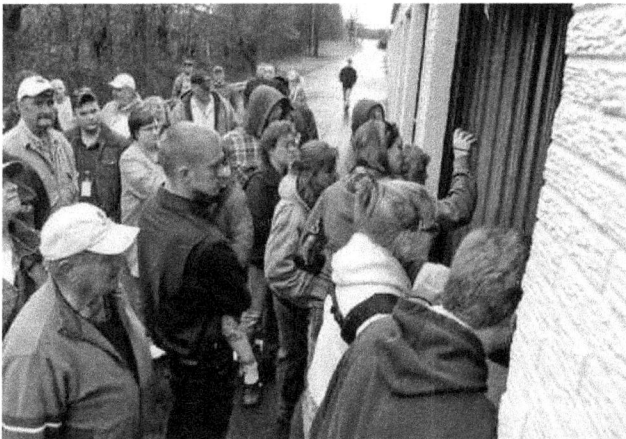

Needless to say the educational institution closed down this system for their surplus disposal. They then started sending all their equipment to the provincial government and it was disposed of through the provincial government auction sales. The equipment was first processed at the educational institution and then sent to the government facility where it was then processed again. This was a very labor intensive process that really did not make much sense to anyone outside the government. This process continued until about a year ago, when brighter minds saw some light.

The educational institution then decided to start sending the equipment directly to the auction houses themselves, cutting out the government middle man. This lasted for some time until just recently when they stopped shipping to the auctions all-together, and just sent the surplused equipment to the recyclers.

As it turns out for them, it was cheaper for them to just send all the equipment to the recyclers and not even try to sell it. To me this made no sense so my friend tried to explain it to me. He said they received all the surplus equipment on pallets from each individual department within the educational institution. For them to sell it, they had to break down the pallets, itemize the inventory, and then transport the equipment to the auction house. All of this took much time, labor, and paperwork to accomplish, not to mention the shipping costs involved. Of course they had to keep track of this because employees were paid to do the work. Then when they got the payments back from the auction company, they could compare the amounts they received to the amount it cost them to process the equipment for sale. Needless to say they were not even covering their expenses. So all they do now is call the recycler to pick up the merchandise and they don't have any of the processing expenses, so it is less expensive for them to just junk the equipment rather than try to resell it. Of course I stepped up to try and solve their problem. I offered to take a number of these pallets off their hands for minimal cost. Amazingly my offer was accepted and we have recently processed over 5 pallets of equipment.

1.7 Setting goals

In this section we are going to talk about setting realistic goals and expectations. In my experience one of the biggest hindrance to achieving great success is the fact that most people set unrealistic goals that can never be achieved. This does nothing more than kill your will to work and you end up with nothing.

This is especially true with people starting out an EBay sales business. They get all caught up in the hype from these shameless US EBay promoters who promise the moon with none of the work. A person gets sucked into buying one of their vastly overpriced courses with the promise that they will start earning thousands of dollars a month with essentially no work because they are going to use a drop shipping system. I have talked multiple times about the old drop shipping scam so I won't waste time doing it again. Instead I want to talk about setting your goals when you first start. If you are just starting out selling on EBay, don't expect to be making thousands of dollars a month. It's possible but not very likely. You need to start small and work your way up to those dollar values. Instead of setting initial goals using dollar values, you are better off setting initial sales number goals such as wanting to sell 10 items in your first

month, then 15 items in your second month, and so on. Then after you have some grounded experience and have sold some items, then you can start setting yourself some monetary goals. **I would suggest starting at $100 a month initially, then working up to $100 a week, then $1000 a month and then $1000 a week, then take the big step and go for $10,000 a month**. Then if everything works out and you have your systems in place, take the big plunge and go for $10,000 a week and enter the big leagues.

There are literally hundreds of different books and courses out there about goal setting and how to use it to your advantage. Rather than reflecting on all the different systems out there, I will give you a couple of tidbits I have found to be useful. First of all I think **your goals should be very specific, and you need to stay away from generalities**. A goal like, I will be successful, is useless. However a goal like, I will sell 10 items is great. Also your goals need to have specific time frames attached to them. When do you want the goal to be completed by? I also suggest setting up 3 different time frames for your goals, weekly, monthly and yearly goals are a great idea. For example, I will sell 10 items this week, and sell 60 items this month, and sell 1000 items within a years' time.

Another thing I suggest is to set multiple goals for the same idea. First of all set your

target goal that you have a realistic expectation of achieving. That is your **TARGET GOAL**. Then look at how you have performed in the past and set a minimum achievable goal based on your past performance. This is a goal that you can generally achieve at least 8 out of 10 times with only minimal work. This is your **MINIMUM GOAL**. Then let your mind go and set a goal that far exceeds your realistic expectations based on your past performance. This is your **OUTRAGEOUS GOAL**. I also suggest doing these three goals for each of your time frames as well. Or mix them up between the two different types. When you use this system you will be very amazed at how many time you actually achieve your target goals, and a few times you will actually achieve your outrageous goals. The when you have a bad month you will still probably be able to at least achieve your minimum goal. And by achieving that minimum you will not be demoralized by not achieving your goals.

What I have proposed above is just a sampling of some goals. It may not be the best system, and it may not be the worst system. Everyone needs to determine for themselves what type of goal system they want to use. The key point here is to use some type of goal system, and once you start doing that you will start to see your success blossom, and you will start to achieve things that you never would have thought possible before.

Buy Local and Sell Global: a value of $49.99

A free Mp3 Audio download that teaches you how to source product locally and sell it internationally for massive profits.
Visit www.FastTrackToEbay.com/book

2   Sourcing Product

For your EBay business to be viable in the long run you're going to need a source of new merchandise to offer once your current stock is exhausted. If you manufacture your own items this should be fairly straightforward; you'll know how much time and effort it takes to create each one and can control your own production rate as necessary. If you're running an existing retail store, you probably have established suppliers already and increasing the supply to account for additional internet sales should generally be straightforward. In other cases, though, your sources of merchandise may be more uncertain.

What follows is a discussion of various ideas and possibilities for where one might find items to sell on EBay. The list is by no means exhaustive, but by the same token you are by no means obligated to explore all of these options. When you find sources you like it can be beneficial to revisit them routinely, allowing you to build up experience and perhaps cultivate a good relationship with your suppliers that could lead to better deals in the future.

2.1 Used goods

Everybody has items they don't need or want any more, but that are in too good a condition to make throwing them away attractive. Most people don't have the means or knowledge to sell them on EBay, however, and this is where you can step in and make money as a middleman. There are probably many local sources where such items are disposed of through sales, and the prices will generally be quite low since there's such a limited customer base available. Consider searching for the following:

2.2 Garage sales

The ultimate in small-scale local-level retail, individual homeowners set up temporary shops in their own garages or yards for a limited time. They're usually only advertised by way of signs posted around the neighborhood, so keep an eye out while you're driving around.

2.3 Flea markets

Sort of like centralized garage sales, flea markets are buildings or even just large

open lots where individual sellers rent booths at low prices to hawk their wares.

2.4 Thrift stores and pawn shops

Thrift stores are themselves a form of middleman much like yourself, purchasing

used items at very low prices and then offering them for sale at merely low prices.

2.5 Estate sales

An everything-must-go form of garage sale in which most of the possessions of a deceased person are liquidated because the new owners have no ability or interest to store them.

2.6 Local live auctions

Auctions existed before EBay, and continue to this day. They are frequently used for liquidations and to dispose of surplus, and if you're the only one present who happens to be interested in buying the items for sale you can get extremely good bargains.

2.7 New items

A wide range of brand new items can also be found at seemingly unreasonable low prices too, if one knows where to look and perhaps is not too specific about one's needs. New items can fetch more on EBay than used ones, even if the used ones are in as-new condition, and some types of items simply cannot be sold if they're used.

Regional crafts, art, gourmet foodstuffs, and the like are often sold locally by the people who produce them. Since the local market for such items is small and since local items are not as "exotic" as those produced farther away, the prices will often be low enough to turn a profit by reselling them online.

Product such as certain books, games and game systems, or movies, sometimes have a cult following in other countries where they haven't been officially released. You may not think anything in your local market would seem "exotic" in other areas of the world, but this could simply be due to long familiarity; if you have opportunity to meet visitors from other countries you might want to ask them about locally-available goods they think might sell well to others at home.

2.8 Local wholesalers

Local wholesalers are the places where local retail businesses go to find new items to sell. The prices charged by wholesaler's leaves room for retailers to add a profit margin and depending on the details of your business this profit margin may be adequate to your needs as well.

2.9 Factories and factory outlets

The next step up the chain from wholesalers, profit margins can be even larger when you buy direct from the producers of the product. The selection can be extremely limited, but since your marketplace is global this may not present a problem.

2.10   Selling non-physical products

Many people still are not interested in handling physical products but still want to sell something on EBay. They ask about drop selling where they do not have to deal with shipping or deal with the products, only the selling. I generally discourage drop shipping scenarios, and have written numerous articles about it in the past.

So now there is another option for selling on EBay, but not selling any physical products. The answer is to sell information. We are in the information age, and information is a valuable commodity, so why not start selling it. There are many reports and eBooks out there, which can easily be sold on EBay. Once the item has been sold and paid for, they can be digitally delivered through email or a website, with little or no cost to the seller. The profit margins are infinite. If you have ever written down any information or written a book, then you can start selling that information online through EBay. This is a major transitional change for most people. What I mean by that is that you are still doing the same work (namely writing

and creating information content) but you are changing the results of your work (selling it online to a much wider audience). For most writers this is a major shift in their thinking, but to the business person this is a major opportunity as well.

<u>The real secret with this strategy is not making a profit from your sales</u>. In fact it might be a good idea to run this process at a break even cost (just to get additional sales), because the true value here is NOT in the profit generated from the sales. The real key here is in getting the contact information from the people who purchase these digital products. In fact what you are doing is building a very valuable lead generation data base. Once someone buys one of your products they become your customer and are no longer a cold contact. You can structure your sale so that they basically opt in to you newsletters and other marketing materials. This customer data can become very valuable for future marketing efforts. In fact, you structure your digital sale products to the advanced products you will be marketing in the future.

As a specific example, you sell reports on how to buy a house when you have no credit. In that report you explain the lease to own concept and how it works. Then later you market your own lease to own deal directly to those people. If the purchasers are not in your local area, then you can do a joint venture with lease to own sellers in other areas. Then you take the purchasers contact info and forward it to a lease to own specialist in the area which they live, either for a fixed lead generation fee or for a piece of the action.

The possibilities for this type of cross promotion are endless, and only limited by your imagination. But still some people don't want to take the time to learn how to do the promotion and EBay sales themselves. These people fall into two categories. Either they are too lazy to learn how to do it themselves or they are too busy with their other business to spend the time doing it. In either case there is a viable option for these people as well. Just hire someone else to do it for you. This is just another form of the old concept of consignment selling. If people are interested in this service please let me know and I can put you in contact with some Buckaru certified sellers who could do it for you.

How to Use eBay for Big Profit$:   a value of $49.99

A free Mp3 audio download with over 60 minutes on why eBay is the optimum business structure to maximize your profits.
Visit www.FastTrackToEbay.com/book

2.11 Summary

These are the techniques I recommend to everyone and which I have taught to Jon and we now do them in partnership with some success (actually a lot of success). In fact we have had such success doing it that CTV news followed us around earlier this year and took about fifty hours of video footage of us at both storage auctions and regular auctions. They also interviewed us a number of times. They finally got it all together and edited the video down to an eight minute segment which aired on the CTV news show called Alberta PrimeTime which aired on CTV2 on October 18th. If you would like to see this segment, you can search it out on the web, or just go to my personal website at www.yakiwczuk.com and see it there.

3   Drop Shipping

3.1 The closely held secrets that EBay course promoters do NOT want you to know!

Today we will talk a bit about the topic of Drop Shipping, and I will let you in on some of the

closely held secrets that EBay course promoters do not want you to know! To start with I will

give you all a brief description of what exactly Drop Shipping is and how it normally works.

Drop Shipping is a very popular sales concept in today's market place, and if done properly can result in huge profits for the sellers. Drop shipping is a process that allows you to sell a large variety of merchandise and no need to carry any inventory at all. In general the

drop shipper is a large manufacture or surplus merchandise liquidator. They generally have much

more merchandise in inventory that they can possible sell or wholesale themselves. They provide

potential sellers information about the merchandise they currently have in stock. This

information would include a description and photo of the individual items and the wholesale

price for the seller. The seller will then use this information to market the items at whatever price they choose to sell it for, the difference between the wholesale cost of the item and the final sale price, is the profit for the seller. Then once the sale is made, the seller forwards the purchasers shipping address and wholesale cost to the drop shipper. The drop shipper then ships the item directly to the purchaser. The seller never has to even touch the item. The benefits of this type of selling are enormous, and result in very little overhead expenses. If done properly drop shipping is the Gold standard for selling on EBay, unfortunately it is very rarely done properly.

Many EBay course packages out there actively promote drop shipping and use that as a dangling carrot to try and sell their particular course. They tell you that if you purchase their course, they will give you exclusive access to their drop shipping warehouses or partners (either for a for free or for an ongoing monthly charge). They will also allow you to use their prewritten item descriptions and photos in your EBay auctions. Some even set this up for you to do with a single click of the mouse. They promote that you now have exclusive access to thousands of different items and that your potential profits are limitless, with very little work and no inventory. If all this sounds too good to be true, well guess what? It is too good to be true! Just use some common sense and think about it for a few minutes. They are selling you this exclusive agreement that will allow you to make 50% profits on every item of theirs you sell. How exclusive is this arrangement, when they are giving this same deal to everyone who purchases their course?

Sure the first person to sell one of their items will easily make 50% profits. But the next day someone else from the program will see that item sold and will say to him-self that he would be happy with only a 25% profit. He then lists the same item, from the same drop shipper, for the lower price. Your only option is to lower your selling price or not sell that item. Then the next day, someone else thinks they would be happy with only a 10% profit, and then someone else thinks that a 5% profit would be fine. Then you get an experienced power seller coming on board and thinking that since he can sell so much volume of that item he would be happy making only 1% profit on each item sold because he will make up for it on the volume he sells. **Suddenly you are now doing all this work and making next to nothing on the sale**. Is this really what you signed up for when you bought your course package? The only people making any money on this situation are the course promoters, and the drop shippers who now have thousands of people selling their items.

The other negative aspect about drop shipping is that you place your entire fate and reputation in the hands of somebody you have never met. After you sell the item, you send the money and buyer information to the drop shipper, and then you hope and pray that they actually send out the item to the purchaser. Since the drop shipper handles thousands of different items you also have to hope and pray that they send out the correct item and that it actually works properly when the purchaser receives it. If there are ever any problems in the process, you are the one the customer will complain too, and you are the one that will get the negative EBay feedback.

Also, when so many people are selling the same items from the same drop shipper, there is no guarantee, that the drop shipper will not run out of merchandise before he gets to your orders. You are then left holding the ball and have to explain to the customer how come they will not be getting the item they paid for.

Educational Grants and Credits: a value up to $3,499.99

We have a special Educational Grant program which helps students with the purchase of Advanced Educational materials. Also any purchase of our related advanced educational programs or products, will result in the same amount returned as a fee credit on a major internet auction site that you can use for various listing upgrades or on site advertising.
Visit www.FastTrackToEbay.com/book

4   Consignment Selling

4.1 Introduction and overview of consignment selling

Many people wonder how they can start selling on EBay, but they don't have any physical products to sell. Well my standard answer to that is that you just need to start a consignment business, such as Jon and Andrea have done. In fact I am pleased to announce that they (EBay ID: kurycats) have become a Buckaru certified consignment seller. That means they have passed my rigorous certification process and I would recommend them as a seller to anyone who contacts me looking for a consignment seller. In fact they do consignment selling for me, and I am very pleased with the work they have done.

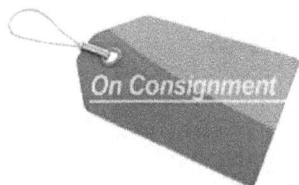

I personally think this is the simplest business in the world to start and make a profit from. **In its simplest form you basically just sell someone else's stuff and take a commission for doing the work**.

Consignment selling has huge benefits. Firstly as the seller, you will have almost no overhead costs. Your costs of inventory will be zero, since you will never have to buy anything to sell, because you are selling someone else's stuff. Also you will not have to keep a large inventory on hand, let your consignors pay for the storage till you get around to selling the item. You will only take possession of the item when you are actually trying to sell it. And you only do this because you will need to take digital photos of the item and write a description of it, and possibly answer questions about the item from potential purchasers. Do not underestimate how beneficial this can be. An average retail sales operation has to pay for a retail storefront, as well as investing thousands of dollars into inventory costs. Many new startup sales businesses cost over $50,000 even before they open their doors. **By doing consignment sales you can literally start your business and start generating income for less than $100**. Your only real cost will be the cost of getting a home based business license, and in a lot of locations that may even be a free expense.

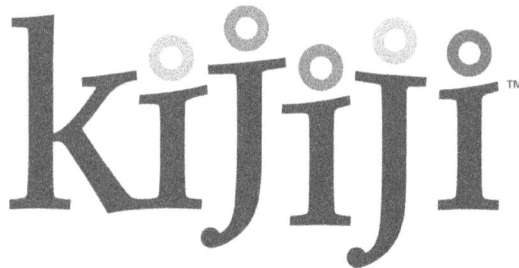

The big question for this type of sales business is where do I sell the items? Of course I am biased and think that EBay is the perfect arena to sell consignment items on. By selling at auction you can have your cash flow starting to come in in less than a week, and if you list the items through an EBay store then you have the cash coming in even sooner (as soon as a potential purchaser sees the item for sale). However EBay is not the only venue to sell consignment items at. I am also a big proponent for using kijiji. This is an online classified add service that allows you to advertise your items locally for free. How much better does that get, now you have zero costs for your advertising expenses, and as soon as you list the item for sale, you may get a potential purchaser contacting you for the sale. Using kijiji it is possible to get cash flow starting the same day you start your selling business. In a lot of areas there are whole networks of people who make a living by selling consignment items on kijiji, why not become part of that world, and work from home on your own hours.

Another great location to dispose of merchandise are local flea markets. These usually run from Friday to Sunday, and you can rent a table by the day, and do not have to be there for the entire time. The rates vary depending on location, but they are generally very reasonable. By renting a spot, you will get a table at the flea market, where you can place all you items out for viewing during the sale times, then you pack up at the end of the day and take your remaining items and profits home with you. Some people who do this very seriously actually get themselves permanent stalls at the flea market. These are the big stalls that look like small stores, and get locked up at the end of the day. They leave their items set up all the time and just lock the entrance to their stall. They literally have a weekend store that they only operate on the weekends, and have their regular jobs during the week.

Finally another great place to sell your consignment items is at a garage sale. In the summer you can set up your own store in your garage and have a number of garage sales on consecutive weekends. That means you don't have to clean up after each weekend sale, you can leave things set up and just open your garage door for the sale. Some municipalities restrict the number of garage sales you can have, but many allow running as many as you like. So in some places like Sherwood Park, Alberta, you can have a garage sale every weekend, even in the winter if you like. It is like having a weekend store in your garage. And if you are selling on kijiji at the same time, have the people come to your house to pick up their items from your garage, they will usually buy at least a couple more items as well.

4.2 How to source items to consign

In this section, we will be looking at sourcing merchandise to sell on EBay or anywhere else. Once you realize that you are able to sell, then why not sell anywhere you want, EBay, internet, flea markets, garage sales, etc.

For your sales business to be viable in the long run you're going to need a source of merchandise to offer once your current stock is exhausted. If you manufacture your own items this should be fairly straightforward; you'll know how much time and effort it takes to create each one and can control your own production rate as necessary. If you're running an existing retail store, you probably have established suppliers already and increasing the supply to account for additional internet sales should generally be straightforward. In other cases, though, your sources of merchandise may be more uncertain.

What follows is a discussion of various ideas and possibilities for where one might find items to sell on EBay. The list is by no means exhaustive, but by the same token you are by no means obligated to explore all of these options. And as a lot of you will realize, these are generally the same places that you will want to sell your items. When you find sources you like it can be beneficial to revisit them routinely, allowing you to build up experience and perhaps cultivate a good relationship with your suppliers that could lead to better deals in the future.

Everybody has items they don't need or want any more, but that are in too good a condition to make throwing them away attractive. Most people don't have the means or knowledge to sell them on EBay, however, and this is where you can step in and make money as a middleman. There are probably many local sources where such items are disposed of through sales, and the prices will generally be quite low since there's such a limited customer base available.

1. **Garage sales.** Are the ultimate in small-scale local-level retail, individual homeowners set up temporary shops in their own garages or yards for a limited time. They're usually only advertised by way of signs posted around the neighborhood, so keep an eye out while you're driving around. Estate sales are just an everything-must-go form of garage sale in which most of the possessions of a deceased person are liquidated because the new owners have no ability or interest to store them.

2. Then there are **Flea markets** which are sort of like centralized garage sales, flea markets are buildings or even just large open lots where individual sellers rent booths at low prices to hawk their wares. Thrift stores and pawn shops are themselves a form of middleman much like yourself, purchasing used items at very low prices and then offering them for sale at merely low prices. They are a great place to find unique items to sell.

3. Another great source of materials are **Local live auctions**. Auctions existed before EBay, and continue to this day. They are frequently used for liquidations and to dispose of surplus, and if you're the only one present who happens to be interested in buying the items for sale you can get extremely good bargains.

These are all great sources for acquiring merchandise to sell; <u>however they ALL have one big drawback to them. You have to buy the items before you can sell them</u>. That takes cash out of your pocket and space out of your life. That's the one big reason why I strongly suggest that everyone do consignment selling. So why not combine the two. When you are looking at any of the above sources, find out from the owners or managers, if they would be interested in having someone do consignment selling for them. Pawn shops and other liquidators may be very receptive to the offer.

4. Now we come to my best source for finding materials to sell on consignment. The secret is **other sellers and in particular other EBay sellers**. Some of the larger EBay sellers have just out grown themselves, and have far too much merchandise on hand to sell themselves so they need other sellers to sell their merchandise. The problem is that they probably do not realize they need the help. I personally know a number of major sellers who are right now looking for help to move their current merchandise. These sellers are actively looking for consignment sellers who they can consign some of their excess inventory to. You may ask why they would do this, but the answer is simple, the more merchandise they sell the more money they make, even if they pay out commissions on the sales. Let's use the cake model. Would you rather have a single cake to yourself, or would you rather have a quarter of the cake, but get it from 10 different cakes? To me the answer is obvious.

Free Bonuses

How to Use eBay for Big Profit$:   a value of $49.99

A free Mp3 audio download with over 60 minutes on why eBay is the optimum business structure to maximize your profits.
Visit www.FastTrackToEbay.com/book

Buy Local and Sell Global: a value of $49.99

A free Mp3 Audio download that teaches you how to source product locally and sell it internationally for massive profits.
Visit www.FastTrackToEbay.com/book

EBay in Canada: a value of $49.99

A free Mp3 Audio download discussing specifics about using eBay in Canada and selling to the USA and the differences between USA and Canada.
Visit www.FastTrackToEbay.com/book

A Millionaire's Mindset: a value of $49.99

A free Mp3 Audio download giving you Insight into the mindset of a millionaire where you will learn a bit about business, real estate and the stock market.
Visit www.FastTrackToEbay.com/book

Fee Credit on Major Auction Site: a value of $49.99

When you register on this major Internet auction site, you will get a fee credit that you can use for various listing upgrades or on site advertising.
Visit www.FastTrackToEbay.com/book

Educational Grants and Credits: a value up to $3,499.99

We have a special Educational Grant program which helps students with the purchase of Advanced Educational materials. Also any purchase of our related advanced educational programs or products, will result in the same amount returned as a fee credit on a major internet auction site that you can use for various listing upgrades or on site advertising.
Visit www.FastTrackToEbay.com/book

5   Dealing with Competitors

Competition is a natural consequence of the free-market system and as a seller on EBay you may initially consider it to be an unfortunate detriment to your business. However, there are some positive aspects to having competitors, and a number of ways that their negative impact on your bottom line can be minimized.

Since sales on EBay are conducted in an open manner, with the records of all recently completed listings available for perusal, competitors who are selling the same sorts of items as you are also conducting "marketing research" that you can take advantage of. By monitoring their listings you can look for what sorts of prices you can expect, what sort of listing practices help sales, and what sort of listing practices hurt sales. Although you shouldn't copy their photos and descriptions verbatim (this would violate their copyrights) you can certainly copy their *strategy* without repercussion.

If you discover a competitor that's doing poorly in some way, this represents an opportunity to out-compete him by correcting whatever error he's making in your own listings. Just as competition may sometimes represent a challenge to your own sales, so too can your own business represent a challenge to your competitors. Your customers will reward you for providing a better service.

There have even been some EBay users who have successfully turned a profit by searching for listings with problems that are likely to reduce their final sale price (misspelled keywords in the title, for example, will prevent many interested buyers from finding the listing), buying the items, and then immediately selling them again with a better-crafted listing. Remember to factor in shipping and other costs if you're considering trying this yourself.

5.1 11 Ways to Out-Compete Other Sellers:

1. **Offer a lower starting price** to entice buyers to cast bids on your listing first. In an auction-based sale system you may even wind up selling for the same price your competitor would have, with your low starting price merely serving to get the buyer involved in your listing rather than your competitor's.

2. Draw your competitor's buyers away with **superior marketing**. This can be as simple as using better keywords in your title or can involve more complex and sophisticated mechanisms such as a well-crafted "About Me" page, an EBay Storefront, or attractive listing templates. More details about marketing are provided in the marketing chapter of this manual.

3. **Offer better performance than your competitors**. This could include accepting a wider range of payment options, a wider range of shipping options, discounts for combined shipping, faster turnaround of their orders once payment is received, and other services such as gift wrapping. Maintaining a good feedback score is also quite important in this respect.

4. **Out-sell your competitor in sheer volume**. If there's little to distinguish your item's listing from your competitors' items listings, but you currently have five items listed for every one item your competitor is listing, odds are you'll receive more sales than he will. The downside of this strategy is that you run the risk of glutting the market and pushing your own prices down.

5. **Pricing** is one of the key variables you can manipulate to influence your sales.

6. **Starting price** – a low starting price entices bidders and generates more interest in your listing, but runs the risk of selling for less than you hoped for if the price doesn't get bid upward.

7. **Reserve price** – protects against having to sell at too low a price while still allowing for the low starting price to draw interest. The downsides are: a) There's an additional fee to add a reserve price to a listing, b) Some buyers are annoyed by reserve prices and avoid listings with one

8. If your reserve price isn't met but the highest bid is in hindsight still acceptable to you, you can use a **second chance offer** to allow the highest bidder to buy the item anyway.

9. **Buy It Now** – an additional pricing strategy, it coexists with auction-style listing. The Buy It Now price is the price at which you're willing to end the auction early, so

Back to list of items   Listed in category: Toys & Hobbies > TV, Movie, Character Toys > Smurfs

Smurfs Collectible. Smurfs Keychain

Buyer or seller of this item? Sign in for your status

Buy It Now Price: **US $1.50**

Buy It Now >

Time left: **2 days 13 hours**
                3-day listing
                Ends Oct-23-03 17:37:01 PDT

Go to larger picture

Location: Muncie, Indiana
                United States /Indianapolis

Shipping and payment details

you should set it higher than you expect you'll get from the auction's bidding. The Buy It Now option disappears once the listing's reserve price is met or, in auctions without a reserve price, once the first bid is placed.

10. **Fixed Price** – similar to Buy It Now but without the option of bidding in an auction-style listing. Buyers will see the listing with a Buy It Now icon and the auction functions disabled. Fixed price listings are similar to how conventional online retail sales are performed, and are most useful when you have multiple copies of the item being listed available for sale.

11. **Best Offer** – an optional feature that can be used with a fixed price listing, this allows interested buyers to offer an auction-like competitive bid. Unlike a full auction, however, each buyer can only submit one best offer and so the price is unlikely to be bid as high.

Free Bonuses

How to Use eBay for Big Profit$:   a value of $49.99

A free Mp3 audio download with over 60 minutes on why eBay is the optimum business structure to maximize your profits.
Visit www.FastTrackToEbay.com/book

Buy Local and Sell Global: a value of $49.99

A free Mp3 Audio download that teaches you how to source product locally and sell it internationally for massive profits.
Visit www.FastTrackToEbay.com/book

EBay in Canada: a value of $49.99

A free Mp3 Audio download discussing specifics about using eBay in Canada and selling to the USA and the differences between USA and Canada.
Visit www.FastTrackToEbay.com/book

A Millionaire's Mindset: a value of $49.99

A free Mp3 Audio download giving you Insight into the mindset of a millionaire where you will learn a bit about business, real estate and the stock market.
Visit www.FastTrackToEbay.com/book

Fee Credit on Major Auction Site: a value of $49.99

When you register on this major Internet auction site, you will get a fee credit that you can use for various listing upgrades or on site advertising.
Visit www.FastTrackToEbay.com/book

Educational Grants and Credits: a value up to $3,499.99

We have a special Educational Grant program which helps students with the purchase of Advanced Educational materials. Also any purchase of our related advanced educational programs or products, will result in the same amount returned as a fee credit on a major internet auction site that you can use for various listing upgrades or on site advertising.
Visit www.FastTrackToEbay.com/book

6   Packaging Techniques

6.1 How to Properly Package an Item for Shipping

Use a new box whenever possible. A previously used box may not adequately protect your shipment, because the more times a box is used, the more it loses its original protective qualities. If you must reuse a box, make sure it is rigid and in excellent condition with no rips, punctures, tears, or corner damage. You also want to make sure that all flaps are intact. Remove any labels and all other shipment markings from the box. Choose a box strength that is suitable for the contents you are shipping. Never exceed the maximum gross weight for the box, which is usually printed on the Box Maker's Certificate on the box's bottom flap. It is important that you cushion the interior contents of your package properly. You must be sure to wrap each item separately. Fragile articles need both suitable separation from each other and clearance from the corners and sides of the box. In general each item should be placed at least two inches (5 cm) away from the walls of the box, and each individual item should be surrounded by at least two inches (5 cm) of cushioning material as well. This will protect your items from the shock and vibration that can be conducted from

the exterior of the box to its contents in transit and also protect from product-against-product damage.

Inflatable packaging (air bags) are not recommended for items with sharp corners or edges and are used primarily as void-fill materials for lightweight items. The problem with them is that extreme hot or cold temperatures may affect the ability of air bags to provide adequate product protection.

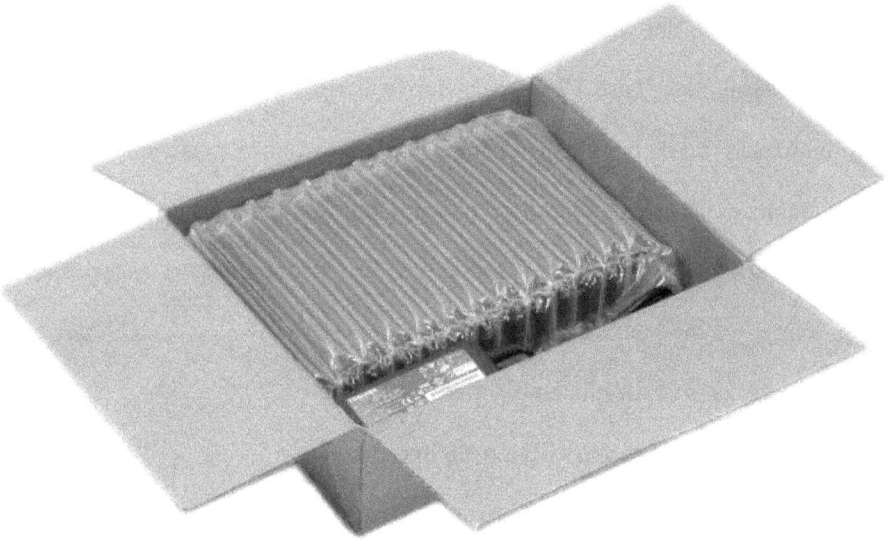

The simplest solution for packaging is Crumpled paper. It must be tightly crumpled, with at least four inches (10 cm) of paper between contents and outer box. It is used primarily as a void-fill material for light-to-medium weight, non-fragile items and items that are suitable for such packing materials. For small or low-density items, crumpled paper is ideal. You can use newspaper for this; separate it into individual sheets and wad each sheet up into a ball, laying down a bed of crumpled paper on the bottom of the box and then filling in around the item after it's placed inside. You can adjust the tightness of the wads depending on the weight and fragility of the item. When the package is finished it should be possible to shake the box vigorously without the item shifting inside, but the sides of the box shouldn't bulge significantly and there should be a little springiness when the sides are squeezed. The only downside of using newspaper is that the ink will rub off on your hands and on the item. It may be best to wrap the item in a plastic bag before packing it to protect it against this.

Shredded paper is generally not a suitable packing material despite how it might seem when you first try padding a box with it. The strips of shredded paper can turn to lie flat, and will do so quickly during shipping. Use shredded paper only for the

smallest, lightest, and most fragile of items.

Styrofoam packing peanuts are easy to use and have good properties for packing a wide variety of items, but they are hard to find second hand and so may be relatively expensive.

When using Styrofoam packing peanuts one must make sure to fill the box tightly enough that nothing can move inside; if the item can shift even slightly during shipping the possibility exists that the peanuts will be able to migrate out from underneath it and the item will settle to the bottom of the box. You may wish to wrap the item in plastic to prevent packing peanuts from getting inside it, depending on whether this might be a problem. Larger pieces of Styrofoam can be obtained second-hand from retailers in the same manner as boxes themselves. One is more likely to find leftover Styrofoam available from stores that sell larger items such as furniture or consumer electronics. Sheets of waste Styrofoam may also be available from building contractors, who use it as insulation. In many ways large pieces of Styrofoam can be ideal for packing larger, heavier items; it provides strong support, it doesn't move around like packing peanuts can, and it can even provide additional structural stiffness to the box. It can take more effort to use it well, however. Styrofoam pieces will likely need to be cut into the right sizes and shapes for your item and the leftover nooks and crannies may need filling with smaller chips of Styrofoam or wads of crumpled paper. Cutting or snapping Styrofoam will release small Styrofoam particles that can be difficult to clean, so you'll almost certainly want to wrap your item in plastic to keep these particles out of it.

Educational Grants and Credits: a value up to $3,499.99

We have a special Educational Grant program which helps students with the purchase of Advanced Educational materials. Also any purchase of our related advanced educational programs or products, will result in the same amount returned as a fee credit on a major internet auction site that you can use for various listing upgrades or on site advertising.

Visit www.FastTrackToEbay.com/book

6.2 Safe Packaging Practices

One of the biggest complaints I have heard from people who buy on EBay, is that when they get their item, it has been broken in transit, or was not properly packaged.

Before we discuss packaging techniques, I am going to relate a couple of stories as to why items need to be packaged properly. It is common knowledge that courier shippers (who wear brown uniforms) are notoriously hard on packages; well here is my personal story on that one. I packaged up a large format computer plotter for shipping. I went a little overboard on the packaging, and used a wooden crate with foam in place Styrofoam as well. To me this looked indestructible. Well not to the shipping company. About 3 weeks after I sent the item, the buyer contacted me and let me know that he had not received the item. I checked with the shipper and they had lost the package, even with their online tracking. Then a couple of weeks later, I got a call from the local shipping office that I needed to come down and pick up the package. I went down to the office and almost fell off my feet. The wooden case was completely gone, there was no packaging material left and the plotter was in small pieces, held together

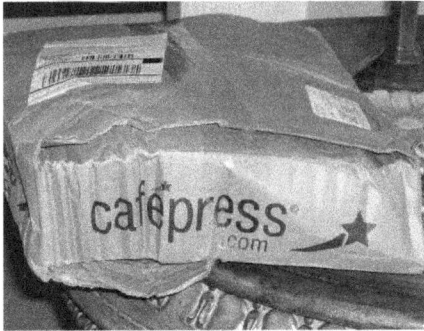

with some plastic wrapping. It looks like it literally fell off the truck and was run over by a number of other vehicles. It was a useless pile of junk. The reason the online tracking lost the package was because the shipping labels were on the box, which was destroyed and lost. I thought, it's all OK, because it was insured. Big mistake. The company refused to give up any insurance claim on the item, and there reason was that it was not properly packaged. I even provided photo proof of the packaged item in an indestructible wooden crate. Their argument was, "OBVIOUSLY the packaging was not good enough, because the item got damaged!! Your fault, no insurance claim!" Granted no amount of packaging would have prevented this situation, but good packaging will prevent most minor damages.

Another fact that most people are not aware of, not even most Canada Post employees, is that **Canada Post has a written policy called a "safe drop". This means that any package they take MUST be able to withstand a drop from a height of 3 feet onto a concrete floor!** YES, you read right, a 3 foot free fall onto concrete! This is a common occurrence in Canada Post sorting plants. All their package conveyor and sorting equipment is at a height of 3 feet, and it is common for the sorting lines to get backlogged and force packages off the conveyor onto the concrete.

At the airport we have all seen those baggage handlers toss the luggage like firewood.

Well they also treat the mail and packages the same way if not worse. I have actually heard stories about shipping company employees who hold contests to see how far they can throw a package without is busting apart. They also are known to keep trophies in their work rooms. The one I heard about was a package which obviously held a glass breakable item. It was smashed and now they used it like a rattle to show newbies on the job how to do things.

I want to point out that these stories are the exception rather than the rule, and that generally most packages get delivered safely and promptly. In reality I have found that less than 2 out of a 1000 packages get severely damaged. Despite all the horror stories we have all heard about Canada Post, I still consider them the safest and most reliable shipper out there. I consider courier services as shippers of last resort, and ONLY use them when an item is either too large or too heavy to go through the postal system.

6.3 Packaging Materials

When it comes to gifts you would rather have not received (but can't just regift it in the family), EBay is the perfect place to do that regifting. There are no worries about your great aunt finding out you gave away that thingamajig she gave. Now sell it on EBay and ship it across the country with no worry about your great aunt finding out about it. And of course you are going to

want to make sure that it arrives and the purchasers in one piece and not destroyed in transit. So today we are going to look at some safe packaging principles. I hope you were all surprised and amazed at how brutal shipping can be.

Ideally the best packaging is the original packaging materials that the item came in, as it will generally hold the item in place fairly well, but it will still need more! Remember most packaging is for items that are generally sold in retail outlets and not shipped across the country through the mail, so you will have to beef up on the packaging. You will probably want to double box it by putting it into a slightly larger box with some packaging between the boxes.

6.4 Sourcing shipping supplies

The vast majority of items sold on EBay are probably best served by being shipped in a corrugated cardboard box. Small shipping boxes are available in most post offices, but they are generally quite expensive and often not as strong as they could be. Since you'll likely be shipping many items it is usually best to look for alternatives.

You may have a collection of cardboard boxes that you've accumulated from items that you've purchased yourself over the years. This will be an excellent opportunity to recycle them. If you have more items to ship than your collection of old boxes can handle, it may be worthwhile to ask around to see if anyone else has a supply they might be willing to give you. Retail outlets often receive their wares in boxes that are subsequently just thrown away, sometimes actually costing the company money to dispose of, so you may find store managers who have large stacks of old boxes they're eager for you to take.

For smaller boxes look for stores that have small, heavy items and a high rate of inventory turnover. Liquor stores, gas stations, and convenience stores are good choices. For larger boxes, consider asking at furniture stores. Don't worry if the boxes you find this way aren't exactly optimal, it's possible to resize boxes with just a little work. You should check with the post office ahead of time and find out whether there are any special restrictions on the dimensions of the boxes that they'll ship.

Try to ensure that any recycled boxes you use are in sound condition, with no major structural flaws. Use a marker to cross out old shipping or inventory labels to avoid confusion. International customs can sometimes reject a package if the box it's shipping in appears

substandard, it may be helpful to wrap the box in a layer of paper to deal with this possibility.

If your boxes are too large for the item in question, it's quite easy to make a box smaller along its vertical axis by cutting down the edges and folding the flaps lower. Cut off the ends of the flaps so that they don't overlap when taped.

If the item is still in its original box, the box may be suitable for shipping directly. However, bear in mind that the surface of the box will receive a lot of abuse during shipping; it will be scraped and scratched, written on with ink, and stickers will be applied at various steps along the way. If the box is in any way valuable it would be best to wrap it in an extra layer of cardboard for protection. The amount of extra space you'll want to leave between the inside of the box and the item you're shipping will vary depending on how heavy the item you're shipping is, how fragile it is, and what sort of packing material you're using. The item should never touch the side of the box directly.

The purpose of packing material is twofold; to fill space and prevent the item from moving around inside the box, and to crush when pressure is applied before the item itself crushes. These two purposes are often at cross purposes since the more crushable the packing material is the less support it can give to the item inside.

For small or low-density items, crumpled paper is ideal. You can use newspaper for this; separate it into individual sheets and wad each sheet up into a ball, laying down a bed of crumpled paper on the bottom of the box and then filling in around the item after it's placed inside. You can adjust the tightness of the wads depending on the weight and fragility of the item. When the package is finished it should be possible to shake the box vigorously without the item shifting inside, but the sides of the box shouldn't bulge significantly and there should be a little springiness when the sides are squeezed. The only downside of using newspaper is that the ink will rub off on your hands and on the item. It may be best to wrap the item in a plastic bag before packing it to protect it against this.

Shredded paper is generally not a suitable packing material despite how it might seem when you first try padding a box with it. The strips of shredded paper can turn to lie flat, and will do so quickly during shipping. Use shredded paper only for the smallest, lightest, and most fragile of items.

Styrofoam packing peanuts are easy to use and have good properties for packing a wide variety of items, but they are hard to find second hand and so may be relatively expensive. When using Styrofoam packing peanuts one must make sure to fill the box tightly enough that nothing can move inside; if the item can shift even slightly during shipping the possibility exists that the peanuts will be able to migrate out from underneath it and the item will settle to the bottom of the box. You may wish to wrap the item in plastic to prevent packing peanuts from getting inside it, depending on whether this might be a problem. Larger pieces of Styrofoam can be obtained second-hand from retailers in the same manner as boxes themselves. One is more likely to find leftover Styrofoam available from stores that sell larger items such as furniture or consumer electronics. Sheets of waste Styrofoam may also be available from building contractors, who use it as insulation. In many ways large pieces of Styrofoam can be ideal for packing larger, heavier items; it provides strong support, it doesn't move around like packing peanuts can, and it can even provide additional structural stiffness to the box. It can take more effort to use it well, however. Styrofoam pieces will likely need to be cut into the right sizes and shapes for your item and the leftover nooks and crannies may need filling with smaller chips of Styrofoam or wads of crumpled paper. Cutting or

snapping Styrofoam will release small Styrofoam particles that can be difficult to clean, so you'll

almost certainly want to wrap your item in plastic to keep these particles out of it.

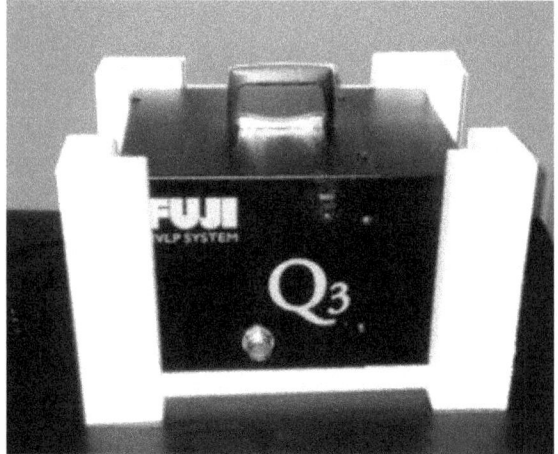

7   Avoiding Scams

To start off this section, we are going to discuss a few things that all EBay sellers should be aware of. And that is various scams that are out there and that unscrupulous buyers can use to scam sellers out of their products or money. For the most part it is very safe to buy and sell on EBay, but all it takes is a few people to screw things up for a lot of others. What I am going to explain to you is very important and every seller should be aware of. Luckily these things are almost never seen, but you do need to be aware of them.

7.1 Shipping an item to a customer

To start with, whenever you ship an item to a customer, **you always want to use a service that will provide you with tracking information and a signature delivery confirmation**. After you send an item sometimes the seller will claim that the item was never received. If that's the case then the seller can make a claim with EBay and PayPal and the judgment will go summarily against you unless you can prove the item was received, and the ONLY way to prove that it was received is if you have a signature confirmation. Signature confirmation shipping is a little more expensive than others but it is definitely worth it especially if it saves you even one charge back because of a non-delivery complaint. Even if you have signature delivery confirmation, you may still get a non-delivery claim filed against you. EBay and PayPal may actually rule in your favor, but to a real scammer, that is not the end of the story. They may then complain to their credit card company. And if they do that you will get what is called a charge back, where the credit card company pulls back their payment from you. When this happens you generally do not have any recourse other than to try and sue the buyer. Generally credit card companies have an unpublicized rule that they will automatically allow a person to file a charge back at least twice a year with no questions asked. Scammers know this and use it to their benefits.

7.2 Overseas shipping scam

Along the same lines as the non-delivery scam is the overseas shipping scam. Overseas buyers may want you to ship by the slowest means possible in order to save money. Even if you use delivery confirmation you may still get scammed. This time it is because surface overseas shipping tends to take 6 to 8 weeks. At the 4 week mark the item is only half way to its destination, and an unsavory buyer may make a complaint for non-delivery. Since PayPal and EBay have a four week deadline for complaints they look at your shipment tracking information and see that it has not received its destination, so any complaint will be ruled against you. Then in a few weeks the buyer gets the item for free. You can try and appeal the claim, but it generally does not work in your favor.

7.3 Buyer requests you to ship to a third party

Another non-delivery scam is when the buyer asks you to ship to a third party, by saying they are buying the item for a friend or as a gift and need it shipped somewhere else. They also may say that they have just moved and have not changed their credit card info yet. Or they may use any number of other stories. Even if you do have signature delivery confirmation you may still get a claim against you for non-delivery. That's because the scammer knows that sellers need to ONLY ship to confirmed payment addresses. And if you do not ship to that confirmed address you leave yourself wide open for a claim against you.

7.4 Not as described scam

The "not as described" scam is more insidious and harder to prevent. After the buyer receives their item, they then make a claim that the item is not as it was described in the auction. They then make a claim and will be reimbursed by EBay or PayPal. The good thing is that they will have to send the item back to you, and that does happen sometimes. But sometimes it doesn't. Also sometimes when the item is sent back to you, you will get customs fees added on, or it may even come as postage due. In a few rare cases the item you get back may not even be the item you sent. I have heard of cases where a rock was sent back, and because you had to sign for the item, the tracking information shows it as being received by you and the buyer gets reimbursed because he returned the item. The rock is an extreme case, but more commonly a different but similar item is returned. The buyer has broken their original item, bought a replacement from you, and then sends you back his broken item.

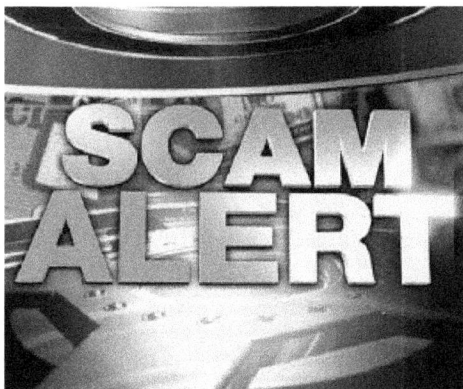

7.5 Protecting yourself as a buyer

Recent Ratings:

		Past Month	Past 6 Months	Past 12 Months
⊕	positive	439	2929	3095
⊙	neutral	1	74	76
⊖	negative	3	58	58

Bid Retractions (Past 6 months): 0

When you find an item on EBay that you want to bid on, there are a number of things you should do before committing to purchase anything from an EBay seller. Some of these things will sound very basic, but you would be surprised how many people do not do them and end up losing money to a scam. The first thing you should do is check the feedback rating of the seller. Their feedback number is that number directly behind their User ID. In general the higher the number the better. Any seller with less than a 100 feedback number will definitely require more scrutiny than if they have a 1000 feedback rating. The next thing to do is to actually look at his feedback profile. To do this you simply click on his feedback rating number and that will take you directly to the seller's feedback profile. Once there, you want to look at how many negative feedbacks they have compared to the positives. Generally any number over 98% positive rating is fine. Don't be totally scared off if you see the occasional negative feedback comment. Even the most experienced and honest sellers will have

the occasional negative feedback, simply because it is almost impossible to please everyone. Generally I will not purchase from any seller who has less than 95% positive feedback rating.

The next thing you need to look at is how many of the sellers feedbacks are from sales and how many are from purchases. One of the tricks some people use is to purchase a lot of low priced items in order to boost their feedback rating, before they start selling. So if most of the feedbacks are from purchases I would be more inquisitive. Actually look at some of the items that the user has purchased, if they are all low priced items under a couple of dollars, then this user probably just tried to boost his feedback and I would be wary of purchasing from them. If his purchases are of significant dollar values then it's more likely he is a reputable user just starting to sell. You also want to check out the items he has previously sold and received feedback for. Look at those items and see if they are consistent with what they currently are selling. If they have been selling inexpensive downloadable eBooks for the last 3 months and they are suddenly listing expensive jewelry or laptops, your spidy sense should start to be tingling!

You also definitely want to check out the other items the user currently has listed. If they have 5 listings for the exact same high priced item, that might be cause for concern. Then also look at their 30 day sales history, and if they have sold the exact same item every week, that might also be a reason for concern.

A classic example of what you should avoid is a seller with a feedback of less than 20 who is selling a laptop computer for half of what it should be selling for. Then when you look at his current and past auctions, you see that he currently has 5 other exact or similar laptops listed and has sold the same items for the last 2 weeks. You would be surprised how many people would send this user their hard earned money and will never see a laptop.

In conclusion I would suggest that **until you are an experienced buyer, you only purchase from high feedback sellers who have a proven track record in their feedbacks**.

7.6 Safe payments: ways that you should NEVER use to make payments!

To start with, we will look at some of the ways that you should never use to make payments with. Of course it goes without saying that you should never pay for an EBay item purchase with cash, unless you are picking the item up in person and inspecting it before making payment. Sending cash through the mail service is never a good idea, as you will have no proof that the payment was actually made. There have been cases where an unscrupulous seller will ask for payment in cash, and then the seller claims to have never received the payment. With cash payments there is no payment tracking available, and becomes one person's word against another's, as to whether payment was actually made. As a purchaser you should ALWAYS be hesitant when dealing with a seller that requires payment in cash.

Other payment methods that should be avoided are instant cash wire transfers such as Western Union or Moneygram services. These forms of payment require the purchaser go to a local western union office and make the payment in the name of the seller. You are then given a money control transfer number which you then give to the seller. The seller can then take this number to any other western union office and collect the payment. This form of payment is quite expensive to make, but is very quick to process and send the money. The down side is that it is exactly like a cash payment and all someone really needs to collect the payment is that money control transfer number. Once the payment is made you have no recourse if you never receive the item.

Of course if the seller will let you pay by check, that is the best methods of payment for the purchaser. When the check is returned to you from the bank you will have a record of where the check was cashed and into what bank account the deposit was made to. If there is a problem with the transaction, you will have proof of payment as well as info on how and when the payment was cashed.

Credit card payments are also a good way to make a payment as you will have all the protection you would normally have with other credit card payments. Unfortunately not many EBay sellers have a merchant account and are able to take credit cards directly.

PayPal™

Probably the best form of payment is through PayPal. PayPal is an online payment processing service that is actually owned by EBay and integrated directly into the EBay auction site. Once you register for a PayPal account, you can then pay for items with your credit card or from your bank account through PayPal. One of the added benefits of using PayPal is that you have additional buyer protection. If there is a problem with the transaction, then you can initiate a dispute directly with PayPal. Possible disputes are if the item is never received or if the item is significantly different than it was described in the auction. Once a dispute is initiated, it will be investigated by PayPal, and could lead to various different dispute outcomes, which may include a refund.

For very high priced items the best form of payment is through an escrow service. An escrow service is a third party service that acts as an intermediary between the seller and the purchaser. Generally the escrow fees are paid by the purchaser. When this type of service is used, the purchaser sends the payment to the escrow service. The escrow service then notifies the seller that the payment has been received and that they should send the item to the purchaser. When the purchaser receives the item, they inspect it and inform the escrow service that the payment may be released. The escrow service then sends the payment to the seller. On the EBay site there are recommendations for their currently approved escrow services. You should only use those services and never use any other services that are recommended by the seller. There have been cases of sellers setting up fake escrow services just to make the purchasers feel safe when in fact it was a scam from the start.

7.7 Surprises and fakes - what to do if the item you receive is NOT exactly what you thought it was

One thing I would like to discuss is what to do if the item you receive is not exactly what you thought it was. This is actually a common problem and occurs more than you would think.

Generally these type of problems are quite minor but annoying. A classic example is that the item you get is a slightly different color than what the photo was. This can occur for a number of reasons and no one is really to blame. Color is a very subjective thing and even though one person describes a particular color, another person would describe it totally

Jimmy Choo's Cutout Bootie $428

Charlotte Russe's Ruched Strappy Stilletos $26.99

differently. Also a digital camera will record colors slightly differently than any other digital camera. Also monitors may display colors slightly differently. So there is no real way to accurately depict the true color of an item. This is a case where close actually does count. If color is really important then you should ask some questions before bidding on the item and confirm exactly what the true color is compared to something of a known color. Also make it clear to the seller that color is an important point, and ask if the item may be returned if it is not the color you thought it was. The seller may or may not allow you to return the item. Don't get to upset if the seller does not want the hassle and asks you to purchase elsewhere.

  If you do get an item that's different, the first step is to go back to the listing and compare it to what was listed. Then politely ask the seller if a return would be a possibility**. Remember that politeness really does count in a situation like this. Being forceful and obnoxious will**

only result in bad feedback and not being able to return the item. I suggest complimenting the seller on the item you received and say that you are sure that he described the item as best he could, but you have a problem with it, and you would like to return it. If possible always allow the other person a way to save face.

I recently purchased an item that turned out to be a fake. Rather than getting all upset with it, I decided to do some research and play the game. I found out that the seller had a previous reputation for selling fakes (yes I should have done that before I bid!), and also refused to take returns. I contacted the seller and thanked him for the prompt shipping of the item. I then mentioned that there was a slight problem with the item and if I could discuss it with him. When he indicated we could discuss the situation, I again thanked him for responding, and then gave him detailed reasons why I think the item he shipped me was a fake. I then told him, I was sure that he did not know it was a fake (when in fact I was sure he knew it was a fake). I told him that the person who consigned the item to him may not have even known it was a fake (I was sure it was his item and not consigned). I then indicated that I really could not use the item since it was for professional use and we could not risk the consequences of using unauthorized materials. **I then indicated that I would like to resolve the situation in some manner that would be acceptable to BOTH of us**. I indicated that shipping the item back to him would just be a waste of money since he could not resell the item knowing now that it was a fake. So I then asked him to just refund a significant portion of the purchase price of the item not including the shipping, and that he should then contact his consignor and get a refund from him. I indicated that that refund would make me completely happy and that I would then leave him a very favorable feedback. After all was said and done I got most of my money refunded and got to keep the fake item. **The whole reason this worked out fine, was because I allowed the seller a way to save face by blaming the whole situation on a fictitious consignor**.

7.8 Spoofing

In this section, we will look at some internet safety issues and what to do if you are targeted by spoof emails.

The Ebay toolbar is an extension produced by Ebay that installs into Internet Explorer, providing a toolbar at the top of the bro wser window that makes many Ebay activities easier and more efficient to perform. The toolbar can be downloaded from http://pages.Ebay.com/Ebay toolbar/ Features include: Customized search for Ebay, Ebay Express, Half.com, and other sites. Quick access to frequently-visited sites such as Yahoo! Mail and My Ebay. Ebay Alerts to notify you before a listing ends or when you get outbid. Perhaps its most important feature, however, is the anti-spoofing protection system "Account Guard".

Spoofing is a technique used by malicious individuals on the Internet to attempt to hijack Ebay or PayPal accounts by creating a web site that appears to be an official Ebay or PayPal site but in reality is owned and operated by the spoofer. There are ways to watch for spoofing that are detailed later in this manual, but the Ebay toolbar makes it much easier by automatically analyzing every page you view and indicating whether it is on a legitimate Ebay or PayPal site by displaying a prominent red or green indicator banner. There are not currently official toolbar plugins available for other web browsers such as Firefox or Safari.

"Spoofing" is the practice of deceiving a person into believing that a website or email they're viewing is from an organization it is not, in order to trick the person into revealing private information or otherwise defraud them. In the case of Ebay and PayPal you should take extra care to watch for such tricks since there is the potential for your finances and reputation to be damaged should your private information fall into the wrong hands.

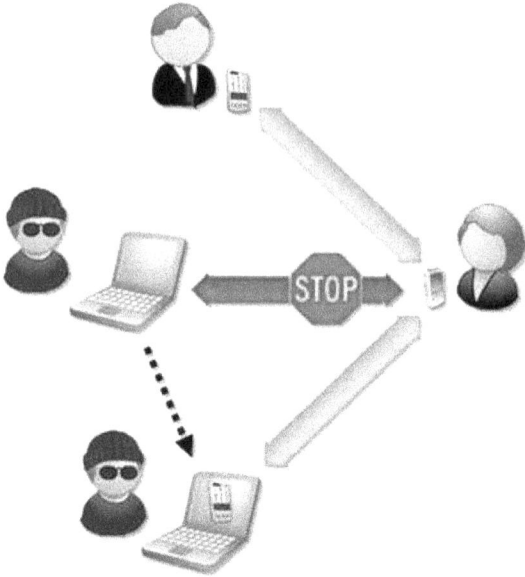

Ebay will never ask for your password in an email or by any other means other than typing it into a password field in a form on the website. If you receive an email that appears to be from Ebay and that asks you to respond with your password, odds are that it's an attempt to hijack your Ebay account. Never give out your password except to type it in to a form on an Ebay web page. Ebay websites always have Ebay.com or Ebay.ca in the url. Other legitimate Ebay-affiliated sites may have the Ebay logo on them, but they will never ask for your Ebay password. Only give your password when asked on one of those two Ebay sites, never give it under any other circumstances.

There are techniques that could allow an attacker to spoof an Ebay website's URL in an email, making it appear that the link you've clicked on is an Ebay site but instead taking you to a website that the attacker controls. If you follow a link from an email to an Ebay page, make sure to check the URL field in your browser to ensure that you've wound up at the page you thought you were going to.

For maximum safety, start each session on the Ebay homepage and follow links from there to reach whatever specific Ebay page you're interested in. If you want to bookmark a specific page somewhere in the Ebay site, make sure you started at the Ebay homepage when getting there.

Getting spoof emails is a common occurrence. Generally the longer you have owned an email account, the more chances that is has been put onto numerous mailing lists. When you do get a spoof email, it is always a good idea to report those emails to the authorities. The easiest way to do this is to just use he forward email function in your email program. For spoof Ebay emails just forward them to the email address spoof@Ebay.com and for spoof PayPal emails, just forward them to spoof@PayPal.com.

7.9 Summary

Most EBay sellers never have any of these situations come up during their sales career. But you should still be aware of them and protect yourself accordingly. Always use signature delivery confirmation with tracking number for all your shipments. Make sure all items get delivered within a short time frame, and always ship to ONLY the confirmed credit card address.

Fee Credit on Major Auction Site: a value of $49.99

When you register on this major Internet auction site, you will get a fee credit that you can use for various listing upgrades or on site advertising.
Visit www.FastTrackToEbay.com/book

8   Selecting a Shipping Company

Shipping companies: either make you a success or drive you into the hole with losses

One of the most common questions I get asked is about shipping, and what shipping company I use. Shipping is one of the most important aspects of running an EBay business, which can either make you a success or drive you into the whole with losses. There is no simple answer to the question of shipping, but I will try to give you some guidelines and what to look for.

In Canada you effectively have 2 different types of shipping available. The first is through Canada Post, and the second is through a courier company such as UPS, FedEx, or Purolator. Each has its own advantages and drawbacks, which we will touch on in this section.

We will start by looking at Canada Post and the services they provide. **In general, Canada Post is one of the cheapest ways to ship an item anywhere in the world**. They provide a number of different shipping options based on speed of delivery. For the EBay seller

the most common option would be the Expedited parcel shipping, and provides a delivery time of approximately 3 to 7 days within Canada and about 10 days to the USA. Another important option with this service is that you can insure your package for up to $1000. Unfortunately you are restricted by the 30 kg weight limit. If you are shipping small items to the USA with a weight less than 1 kg then there is a special category called small packet shipping available, unfortunately on this service you are restricted to a $100 insurance value, and has roughly the

same transit time as the expedited parcel. Also unfortunately there is no small packet rate for shipping within Canada. This is a very frustrating situation, since it can mean that for small lightweight items it is far more expensive to ship it within Canada than to send it anywhere else in the USA or the world. Most Canadian customers do not realize this and it needs to be explained to them. If your items need to be delivered within a faster time frame then Canada Post also offers a service called Xpresspost. Although it has a much faster delivery time, it is also about twice as expensive as the expedited parcel. **Generally I have found that the Xpresspost service is generally not worth the extra expense it costs, and there is really no guarantee that the package will arrive there any faster.**

When shipping elsewhere in the world, Canada Post offers both surface and air parcel services. The expected transit time for a surface parcel can be up to 6 to 8 weeks, and the air parcel is about 10-14 days. However the air service is about two to three times the cost of the surface service, and effectively there is no guarantee that it will be any faster. **We have found that the surface parcel is still the best way to ship, but you must inform your customer about the 6 to 8 weeks expected transit times**. Again for small lightweight packages (under 2 kg) there is a special small packet rate, for either surface or air shipping. These small packet rates are actually a very cost effective form of shipping. Canada Post also offers the Xpresspost service for overseas shipping. And as you would expect it is a very pricey way to ship, but it is the quickest service they have. There are also additional weight and size restrictions when sending to certain overseas countries.

In general, courier services such as UPS and FedEx tend to be much faster than the postal services but they are also quite expensive. Also these forms of shipping generally require much more documentation to be filled out. In general the only advantage that we have found with couriers is that they have a much higher weight and size limit on the packages they will ship. For example UPS has a 150 lb limit for its packages. Couriers will also sometimes allow you to ship a package freight collect. This is where you ship the package to the customer without paying for the shipping upfront. The customer is charged the actual shipping cost by the courier when the package is received. This sounds like a great way to ship but it does have its drawbacks. In rare cases the package is delivered and the charges are not collected (or the customer refuses to pay the charges). Then the shipping company will come after you the shipper for the cost of the shipping, and you have effectively no recourse.

In general we have found that courier shipping is only useful for large heavyweight items that cannot be sent through the postal services. For us the shipper of choice for all destinations is the Canadian postal service.

9 Taking Action!

9.1 Making a decision and taking action

For a moment, we are going to go totally off the topic of EBay, and into what I consider the most important aspect of any business or investment venture you are ever going to get involved with. And that is the concept of **making a decision and taking action**. They may sound like two totally different concepts but in reality they are actually the exact same concept! It is said that all successful people make a decision within the first 30 seconds of hearing about an opportunity, and I truly believe this. If you can cultivate the ability to make a decision and take immediate action you will ultimately become successful in whatever you do.

When I am at an auction and purchasing items to sell on EBay, I use this concept constantly. At a live auction you need to make instantaneous decisions about an item. If you stop to think about it, even for a few seconds, the item will be sold to someone else, and you have missed your chance.

Here is an example from real life. I was recently at a weekend seminar presentation where they were giving away cruise packages as door prizes valued at $800 to $1000. Everyone in the room was gaga over the prizes and everyone wanted one because they were so valuable. At the end of the first day I was talking with other people at my table and told them they would really be surprised if I were to win the door prize because I do not like to travel. I told them that I would offer the prize to the first person to give me $200 cash! Everyone laughed, and everyone at the table indicated they would gladly give me $200 for the cruise, but I knew they were really thinking "Oh sure he would (sarcastically)." Well guess what happened the next morning. They did an on time prize drawing and the prize a cruise for 2, and guess whose name they drew. That's right they picked my name. After the obligatory yelling, and screaming, I ran up to the front, accepted the prize. Then as I took the first step away from the presenter I stopped dead, looked at the audience and yelled out, "I don't like to travel, so the first person with $200 cash in my hand will get the cruise!" The seminar presenter was just so

startled that he was speechless for a few seconds (and if you know this presenter, you know he is NEVER speechless). Well this turned out to be a classic case where people just refused to take action, even when everyone wanted this prize. By lunchtime NO ONE had approached me yet to claim the prize! I seriously thought it was going to go to waste. Then timidly one lady approached me and asked if I still had the prize and if I was serious about what I said. I told her I could not believe no one had claimed it yet. She gave me the $200 and was ecstatic about getting the cruise package. And the clincher was that she was an inner circle member and the only reason she took action was that she had recognized me from other events. And as it turned out she was the ONLY person to approach me about the offer. Can you believe it? Out of 200 people in attendance (every one of them wanted the prize), and I was offering it to them for 25% of value and no one else could be bothered to take any action. My congratulations go out to that brave lady who took action and is now cruising the Caribbean.

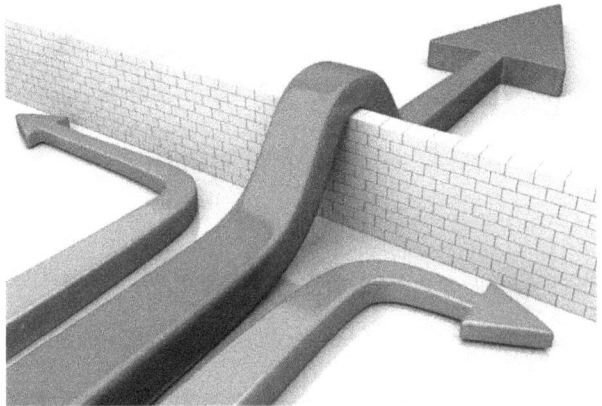

Remember in most cases it does not matter if the decision you make is right or wrong, the important thing is that you made a decision. If you are right, then great. If you are wrong, then you can do something to correct the problems. It is the procrastination that generally kills you, or eats the life out of you.

9.2 You can never please everyone

As a seller one of the most important things you need to learn, is that you can never please everyone! We recently experienced this. We had a customer who bought a few items and then got upset with the total cost of the shipping. He waited till he got the items and then he was impossible to please and went so far as to demand all his shipping costs back. The end result was that we ended up with a bunch of negative feedback because he left it for each item he purchased. Luckily EBay only recognizes it as a single

negative when calculating the feedback percentages. He was a low feedback purchaser, so we could not research his feedback rating prior to the auctions closing. If you ever have concerns about a purchaser, I suggest that you cancel their bids and then immediately place them onto your banned bidder list so that they cannot bid on your items. Sometimes you just have to put up with the garbage, and accept the fact that you cannot please everyone. The moral of this story is that **sometimes you just have to accept things and move forward**. Don't let it eat you up and paralyze you from moving forward.

9.3 Follow-through

In this section, I am going to talk a little bit about follow through and determination and the results of those actions. To start with I want to tell you a story that started about a year ago at the real estate weekend. While I was there I talked to a lot of people about EBay and what it could do for you. We will start with the sad side of the story first. A few people approached me about learning more about selling on EBay and they offered to come and help me out. I said great and that we should meet for a lunch to talk about it further. We set up a time and place for a lunch meeting and then to my surprise I was actually stood up for that meeting and never heard from those people again. Not even an email explaining why they never showed up. I subsequently saw them at other events and never even got an apology for missing the meeting. I found out that since that time, things have not gone well for them financially and they are on the verge of bankruptcy. Personally I think their actions with me were a good indicator of things to come for them.

Another person who actually met with me afterward took a further step. They seemed to have initiative and be someone I could trust. I decided to test them and gave them a few items to sell on EBay to see how they would do. My intent was to have them be a consignment seller for me, where I could provide them with items to sell on EBay. Well after a month of not hearing from them, I tried to track them down to find out how they were doing. Well my emails were never returned and neither were my phone messages. To this date I have never heard back from them, and have not received back any of the items I gave them to sell.

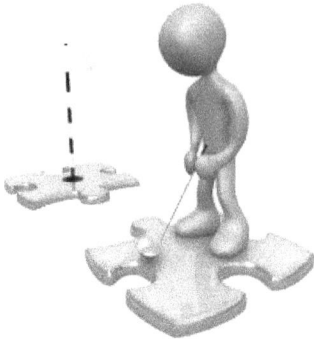

Now on to the success story. While I was talking to some people at the Real estate event a young couple stood patiently in the back ground waiting to talk to me. I guess they waited about 20 minutes before finally jumping in and talking to me. We had a good discussion and followed it up with a lunch meeting. They showed up for that meeting on time and followed it up with some other communications. They then offered to work for free. They did what they said they were going to do so I decided to take the next step with them and give them some items to sell on EBay. They took those items and kept me informed on what they were doing. I helped them out any way I could and things progressed. Again after a few months they proved themselves by doing what they said they were going to do and kept in close contact with me asking for advice and guidance. Now after a year of working together I am proud to consider them very close friends and great business partners. Jon and Andrea are the founders of Kurycats Auctions and now have a thriving EBay auction business. Jon recently quit his full time job to concentrate on the business.

Through my guidance and the information in my EBay course package they were able to recoup the entire cost of the EBay course within the first 3 months of their consignment business. Then in the fourth month they made more than the first three months combined. And that was with only one consignor. They now have many more consignors and are growing their business beyond belief.

That is the power of follow up and commitment. They did what they said they were going to do, and then followed up with the things they did. They started their journey by working for free, and anyone who does that is bound to be a success in anything they do.

Fee Credit on Major Auction Site: a value of $49.99

When you register on this major Internet auction site, you will get a fee credit that you can use for various listing upgrades or on site advertising.
Visit www.FastTrackToEbay.com/book

Free Bonuses

How to Use eBay for Big Profit$:   a value of $49.99
A free Mp3 audio download with over 60 minutes on why eBay is the optimum business structure to maximize your profits.
Visit www.FastTrackToEbay.com/book

Buy Local and Sell Global: a value of $49.99
A free Mp3 Audio download that teaches you how to source product locally and sell it internationally for massive profits.
Visit www.FastTrackToEbay.com/book

EBay in Canada: a value of $49.99
A free Mp3 Audio download discussing specifics about using eBay in Canada and selling to the USA and the differences between USA and Canada.
Visit www.FastTrackToEbay.com/book

A Millionaire's Mindset: a value of $49.99
A free Mp3 Audio download giving you Insight into the mindset of a millionaire where you will learn a bit about business, real estate and the stock market.
Visit www.FastTrackToEbay.com/book

Fee Credit on Major Auction Site: a value of $49.99
When you register on this major Internet auction site, you will get a fee credit that you can use for various listing upgrades or on site advertising.
Visit www.FastTrackToEbay.com/book

Educational Grants and Credits: a value up to $3,499.99

We have a special Educational Grant program which helps students with the purchase of Advanced Educational materials. Also any purchase of our related advanced educational programs or products, will result in the same amount returned as a fee credit on a major internet auction site that you can use for various listing upgrades or on site advertising.
Visit www.FastTrackToEbay.com/book

10 Advanced Strategies

10.1   Expanding your EBay business

In this section, we are going to talk a bit about expanding your online sales business. I have talked a bit about this in the past and told everyone how my partner Jon has opened up a physical consignment store to work right alongside his online EBay sales business. Now I am going to talk about expanding even further. Also in the previous sections, I have talked about sourcing merchandise from local auctions where you can get screaming good deals on almost any sort of merchandise. Well this section is going to roll all of that into a single concept. That concept is to expand your online auction business with a real live auction business. I have done just that, and I pleased to announce here in this article, that Buckaru Auctions is now a live auction business and we are able to hold and host live auctions in addition to our online sales. For the last little while, both my partner Jon and myself have been attending auction school to learn how to do live in person auctions, and just last week we graduated and are now fully accredited live auctioneers. We hope to be holding our first live auction sometime very soon in the Edmonton area.

By adding a live auction component to your business you will actually capitalize on a number of different areas. First of all, you will now have an outlet to dispose of the merchandise that is not appropriate to sell online though EBay, such as furniture and common household items as well as low value items. Next you will also have people bringing you items to sell. As most of you know I have always encouraged the concept of consignment selling as a great way to source merchandise to sell. **Well with a live auction, people will be bringing you their merchandise to sell in droves. You can now sell their merchandise online or through the live auction, or even through your store if you have expanded that way**. Having a live auction is literally a license for people to bring you their stuff to sell.

Now we will either sell peoples stuff through online auctions, live auctions, through the consignment store, or we will just come right out and purchase the merchandise from them for cash. We are now a one stop location for people to get rid of anything they may have that has some value. Also other auction houses will also do business with you and you can now buy directly from them so that in a lot of cases, surplus product will never be offered to the public. I was surprised to find out how many deals are done behind the scenes in between auction houses. We recently picked up 2 pallets of computer systems and our average cost was $1.50 per computer system!

The other great thing about live auctions is that they have a very quick turnaround time. You can have a whole warehouse full of merchandise sold within a day, and the warehouse emptied out the following day, and made up to 50% or more on everything that was sold. The average auction house will take consignments for 30 to 50% so let's use an average of 35%. Then at sale time most auction houses charge a 15% buyer's premium. This is an additional cost that a purchaser must pay just for buying an item at auction. It is a very common occurrence and almost everywhere is going to this model. So with the 35% commission and the 15% buyer's premium the auction company is making 50% without having to buy anything or outlay any money upfront for inventory. It is one of the most lucrative businesses ever devised.

Free Bonuses

How to Use eBay for Big Profit$:   a value of $49.99
A free Mp3 audio download with over 60 minutes on why eBay is the optimum business structure to maximize your profits.
Visit www.FastTrackToEbay.com/book

Buy Local and Sell Global: a value of $49.99
A free Mp3 Audio download that teaches you how to source product locally and sell it internationally for massive profits.
Visit www.FastTrackToEbay.com/book

EBay in Canada: a value of $49.99
A free Mp3 Audio download discussing specifics about using eBay in Canada and selling to the USA and the differences between USA and Canada.
Visit www.FastTrackToEbay.com/book

A Millionaire's Mindset: a value of $49.99
A free Mp3 Audio download giving you Insight into the mindset of a millionaire where you will learn a bit about business, real estate and the stock market.
Visit www.FastTrackToEbay.com/book

Fee Credit on Major Auction Site: a value of $49.99
When you register on this major Internet auction site, you will get a fee credit that you can use for various listing upgrades or on site advertising.
Visit www.FastTrackToEbay.com/book

Educational Grants and Credits: a value up to $3,499.99

We have a special Educational Grant program which helps students with the purchase of Advanced Educational materials. Also any purchase of our related advanced educational programs or products, will result in the same amount returned as a fee credit on a major internet auction site that you can use for various listing upgrades or on site advertising.
Visit www.FastTrackToEbay.com/book

11   FAQ

Can you display photos?

Yes you definitely can display photos, and I recommend that everything you listing contains actual photos of the item you are selling. Do not use existing web images of the item but take your own photos of the item and use them. EBay provides a service that will host your first image for free, and then charge for any additional photos. Alternatively if you have web space available all you have to do is include the web address in the listing and your photo will be seen, and you won't be charged any fees from EBay.

What product requirements do you look for?

Generally I will consider selling any type of product on EBay. My general requirements are that the item is less than 30kg and generally smaller than a breadbox. The only reason for this is because my preferred method of shipping is Canada Post and they have size and weight limitations on the items you can ship through them. Couriers allow for larger and heavier items.

What type of products would you market on EBay for the most potential profit?

This is a good question that unfortunately does not have any specific answer. The main key factor for your profit potential is the price you pay for your item. If you are able to purchase your products cheaply enough, then you are going to make a good profit on them. Another way to increase your profit is to specialize on items that are hard to find. Personally I suggest that people add value to their items by providing expertise. If you are familiar with let's say antiques, then you should include information on how you graded the item and how it compares to other similar types of items, and why this item is worth more than the others. There is GREAT potential for anyone who is willing to arrange shipping for LARGE and HEAVY items. This market is untapped, as most people do not want to bother with the work. If you are buying at local auctions, the big bulky items tend to go very very cheaply because nobody wants them, and nobody wants the hassle of shipping them!

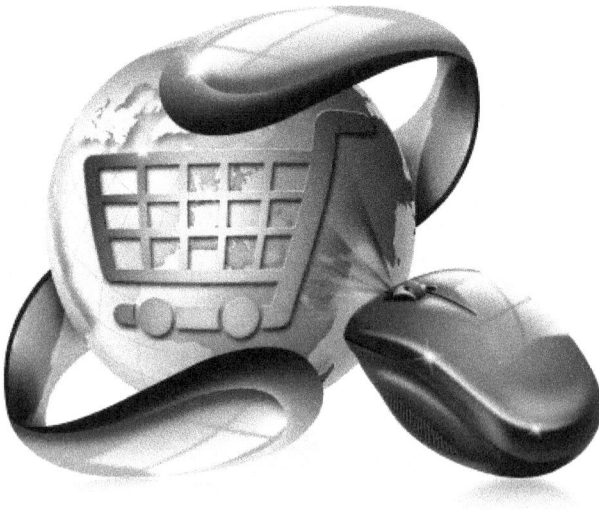

Do you do consignment selling?

Unfortunately I no longer do consignment selling, only because I have out grown that aspect of the business. I actually consign all my items to another seller. If you are interested in consigning with him as well, then please get in touch with me and I can put you in contact with them. Consignment selling is a GREAT way to source products to sell on EBay without the expense of building up inventory. If the items don't sell, you just give them back to the consignor all you are not out anything. If the item sells you get a thick percentage of the sale price for your expertise. There are actually companies now that sell Franchises for doing consignment selling on EBay, and they sell for upwards of $25,000. Learn to do it yourself for a fraction of the cost (Hint: check out our EBay course package).

How much do I need to invest?

Practically you can get started selling on EBay for almost nothing. The only practical requirement is that in order to register for a selling account, you need to have a valid credit card so that any fees you rack up can be charged to that card. Once you list an item for sale, EBay charges you a small fee for that listing (from $0.25 to a couple of dollars depending on the starting price of your item). So if you list 10 items with a starting price of $9.99 your total listing fees would be only $2.50. Then there are also some nominal fees once the item sells and they are a small percentage of the final sale price. And all those fees are only charged at month end, and by that time you should have already received payments for the items you have sold. I usually list items on 7-day auctions, which means you get cash flow starting in 7 days.

How much inventory do you keep?

I personally keep a large inventory, but that is NOT the norm. If you specialize in consignment selling, then you won't have to keep any inventory. Once you start selling, you will generally find that your inventory will slowly build by itself without you really noticing it. When you find a good priced item to sell, rather than just getting one of them, you will end up buying a bunch of them and then just use the same listing over and over again to sell your multiple copies of that item.

How do I get started?

Just make the decision to start selling, and start doing it. Getting a little bit of education will

definitely give you a jump-start over the masses.

Fee Credit on Major Auction Site: a value of $49.99

BONUS

When you register on this major Internet auction site, you will get a fee credit that you can use for various listing upgrades or on site advertising.
Visit www.FastTrackToEbay.com/book

Are there any tricks to save $$$ on shipping?

The simple answer to this is YES. Generally your postage costs are determined by size and weight of the package and there is no real way to save on those other than picking a different transport company. I have found that Canada Post is generally the least expensive, and most reliable. Courier companies are the most expensive and generally have hidden costs. However you can really save money by using recycled packing supplies rather than buying them new each time.

Are there companies willing to let you sell their products on EBay and do the shipping so you don't have to?

This is called drop shipping and I have talked and written about this a number of times. To do this type of selling properly you need an EXCLUSIVE agreement with the supplier. If you can get an EXCLISIVE agreement, then this is the absolute best way to sell products online. If you are just one of many people doing this for the same supplier, then everyone will be trying to sell for less and your profit margin will shrink to nothing, and you will end up working for less than the minimum wage. This leads right into the next question.

Is "St*Online" a legit company?**

Many companies like this exist, but look closely at what they are trying to sell you. Many of these companies use EBay to get you in the door, and then try to upsell you into buying their website building products or e-commerce services and then tell you that it is better to use EBay for advertising and drive customers to the website they provide you. We will discuss this in the next question. These companies generally make their money by providing you the websites and then continue making money off you each month for the fees they charge for hosting and support of the website. I personally know people who have paid these fees for a number of years (because they set it up to automatically debit you bank or credit card) and have never made a dime from their website. The other services these types of companies promote are drop shipping services. They say that for the fee that you pay them, they will give you access to a vast network of warehouses of products for you to sell. They will even provide you with the descriptions and photos of the items. All you have to do is sell the item for them and keep your profit. Yah, right! Good story! How many thousands of people do you think they have doing this already? It is a great deal for them. They get thousands of workers to sell their products and empty their warehouses. The people end up working for less than the minimum wage, AND these people pay them huge amounts of money for the privilege!

Can I link my website to EBay and just sell off my website instead?

The answer to this is "sort of". The only place you can link to your website on EBay is on the "Aboutme" page. Any links within an auction listing to an outside website are in violation of EBay listing policies and you can be suspended from selling for it. You can be sure that if any of your competitors who look at your listings find any links in there, they will definitely report you to EBay for listing violations and get you kicked off the site.

What is the best way to manage multiple listings?

Initially using the MyEbay page on the EBay site should be sufficient for most people. Just using those free resources you can manage quite a few listings at once. Once you become a significant powerseller and are managing a couple hundred listings a month, then you will probably want to investigate some form of auction management tool. Each tool has their own pros and cons, some tools are online and some run off your own computer. EBay provides a number of premium auction management tools and there are also a number of third party applications as well.

How do I find the item I am looking for or need?

Even though this sounds like a bit of a ridiculous question initially, it is actually a very relevant question given the number of items listed for sale on EBay. The EBay website

actually has a very powerful search tool built into it. All you need to do is put in a keyword for the item you are looking for, and it will search the entire site for items matching your keyword. If you don't get any hits on the words you entered, then you can use the advanced search and it will search all the text within the listing, instead of just the listing titles. If you get to many hits, then you can narrow down your searches to specific categories, or perform further searches using only the results from the first search. You also search by item sellers or various other adjustable criteria.

What steps should one take to feel comfortable before bidding on an auction?

The first step is finding an item that fits what you are looking for. The next thing to do is to research the seller of the item. First look at his feedback number. The higher the number the more transactions they have completed. Next look at his feedback profile, and see how many comments are from sellers, and how many comments are from buyers. If you are buying from this person, you want to concentrate on the comments from other purchasers. Look at how many negative comments they have received from other users on previous transactions. Don't be put off, if you see an occasional negative, as it is very hard to please everyone all the time. Next look at the actual feedback comments to see what people say about the transactions. Next look at the other auctions the user currently has listed. If they have multiple identical auctions, you might want to enquire as to the reason, before bidding. Finally look at the user's completed auctions, to see if he has sold the same item before. If they have, you may wish to find out how come they are reselling the same item over again.

What is the best way to pay for the item I won at auction?

As a buyer my opinion is that the best way to pay for an item is to probably use PayPal. It is integrated directly into the EBay system, and you can fund the transaction from either your credit card or your bank account. It also allows you to pay immediately after the auction has ended and results in your item getting shipped out faster. PayPal also offers you some buyer protection features discussed earlier in this eBook. This is important if there is a problem with the transaction. Other acceptable forms of payment would be by check, money order, or bank draft, but remember that the payment will take time to be received by the seller. I never recommend that people use cash to pay for an EBay purchase and under no circumstances should anyone ever send cash through the mail system. Even if you pick up the item in person, I don't recommend using cash. If there ever is a problem with the transaction there is no record of your payment ever being made.

The seller of an item wants me to send him the payment by Western Union wire transfer, what should I do?

As a buyer I would never recommend sending any payments by Western Union or Moneygram. These are wire transfer services and offer NO protection to you the buyer. It is the exact same thing as sending cash. You take cash to a Western Union office, and give them information about who and where the money is going. They then give you a money control transfer number. You then need to email that transfer number to the seller. Then all the seller needs to do is enter any Western Union office anywhere in the world and present that number to them. They will then give that person the money in cash. Because all the seller needs is that number to claim the payment, it is a very anonymous method to get money, which is why most scammers require that payment be made by these methods. Also the costs for using these services are very expensive.

If I buy something and it is not what was advertised, or I don't get it, what can I do?

The first thing to do would be to contact the seller, and discuss the problem with them. Most disputes can be easily resolved as most sellers are very reasonable. If you cannot come to a satisfactory resolution, EBay has a number of dispute processes that may be initiated. Ultimately you may leave that seller a negative feedback comment, which will remain as a permanent record on his profile. If you used PayPal for the payment you may also initiate a PayPal dispute. If the PayPal dispute is ruled in your favor then you will be refunded your payment. The exact process is a little more complicated and not appropriate for a quick short answer.

Should I use a separate ID to purchase items?

This is a personal preference, and generally depends if you are a major seller using EBay for a business or somebody who is just playing around. Most professional sellers set up separate ID's for the items they sell and the items they buy on EBay. That way it keeps the two activities separate and distinct. Any negative comments you receive from problematic buyers will not hurt your buying reputation, likewise any comments you get from problem sellers will not hurt you selling reputation. This method also allows you to purchase cheaply priced items on EBay and then resell them for a profit also on EBay, without anyone finding out where you got the items from.

Should I pay extra for expedited shipping?

Again this is a personal preference and would ultimately be determined by how fast you need the item. Remember that most sellers only ship out items once or twice a week, so there may be a few days of lag time between the time you pay for the item and the time it's shipped out. This lag time may be longer than the time you save by using the expedited shipping, so there may not be any benefit to it. You must also remember that most shipping companies do not guarantee shipping transit times. Even though they offer different rates and suggested transit times, there is NO guarantee that those times are accurate. Also remember that if the items are crossing a country border there may be unexpected delays through customs. In my own personal experience I have found that in general it is not worth extra expense for expedited shipping.

What is the best method to have items shipped to me?

My personal favorite shipping service is the good old postal service. If you get sent an item using a courier service, then there is a good chance that you will be hit with some unexpected or hidden fees after you have received the item. If the items come across the border then the courier service must do extra paperwork and collect the GST for the item. For this small amount of work they charge a customs brokerage fee in addition to their normal shipping costs. Generally these fees are at least $20 USD, not counting any duty or taxes that may also be collected or due. The problem here is that you do not find out about these costs till after you get the item. You either have to pay the amount when the item is delivered (if you don't pay the delivery person then you don't get the item) or you get an unexpected bill a few weeks after the item arrives. The postal service generally only charges $7.00 for the same service, and sometimes they forget to do that.

How do escrow services work?

This is a payment method that is very useful for high priced items and offers good security to both the buyer and seller. The buyer sends his payment to the escrow service. Once received the escrow service tells the seller they have received the payment and that the seller should then send the item to the purchaser. Then once the purchaser receives the item, they can inspect it and then inform the escrow service that the item has been received and is satisfactory. The escrow service then sends the payment to the seller. The only concern with this payment method is that you use a respectable escrow service for the process. In the past there have been cases where fraudulent sellers have set up fake escrow services to handle fake transactions and scam the purchasers. EBay has a page with recommended escrow services and those would be the only ones I would use.

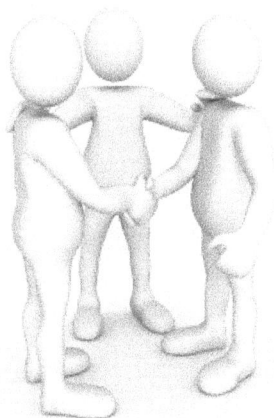

What are the best days and times to start and end EBay auction listings?

Personally I think there is no real correct answer for this. Many people and companies have claimed to do research as to when be the best time to start and stop auctions, but I think common sense is the best guide. To start with you are selling all around the globe so if somebody tells you that the best time to start an auction is 7pm; it really does not matter when you start it, because it will be 7pm somewhere in the world! Even if you are only considering selling in North America or just in Canada, you still have 4 or 5 time zones to deal with. Rather than looking at specific times look at the bigger picture. If you are selling items that are more business related, then start and end your auctions during business hours because that's when the business people will be looking at them. For personal use items start and end them in the evenings or on the weekends. But remember that a lot of people also follow their personal items while they are at work and working people will also follow their business items when they are at home. So again the times really don't matter. So my recommendation is to just forget about starting or ending your items at any set times, start and end you items at the times that are MOST convenient for you the seller!!!

Do you have a recommendation as to starting prices for an auction?

There are many different thoughts on this factor on an auction. The thinking goes that you should always start your auctions for a very low price, and let the market and bidding frenzy drive up the price. The low price grabs every ones attention and once someone starts to bid on the item, they get hooked on it and continue bidding because their ego will not let them get out bid and loose the item. You have to remember that this only works for items that have a wide appeal or large market demand. For low demand items, you may only get a single bid on it and it will sell for its starting price and you get shafted! That's why my thinking is to start your auction at the price you want to sell the item at. That way as soon as you get a single bid on the item, you will have the sale at the price you want. Anything above that price is pure gravy on top.

How do you factor in shipping costs?

This is totally up to the seller. Some sellers include the shipping costs as part of the item prices; because they think that will attract more bidders (they just effectively increase the starting price for their item). But personally I think that doing that actually drives bidders away, because most people just do their searches by bid price and don't really pay attention to the shipping cost till after they have won the item. So if you include shipping into the bid price, your item will show up lower in the searches and it will be less likely to be bid on. Generally all shipping costs are added on to the final bid price for the item, after the auction is completed. You determine the shipping costs beforehand and then they are stated in the listing.

About the Author

Hi there, my name is Larry Yakiwczuk. I am the founder and owner of Buckaru auctions and Buckaru investments. I have six university degrees, 25 years of real estate investing experience, 10 years' experience trading derivatives, and have been financially free for the past 10 years.

I started buying and selling merchandise while I was still at university back in the early 1990's. I attended my first auction in 1993 and got a rare computer part for $10 that was easily worth over $500. That is the moment I became hooked on auctions. After that I attended a lot of garage sales and a lot of auctions. I started acquiring so much stuff that I did not know what to do with it. My garage is full, my basement was full, and I needed to do something. That's when I started holding garage sales myself. I had some of the largest garage sales in the area. People waited all year to come to my garage sale. I used to advertise them in the Bargain Finder and was singly responsible for them changing their advertising system. Rather than just running free ads like everyone else, I would actually pay for them. They used to charge $5 for an upgrade from their free ads. I would combine all of their upgrades together, so for $20 I ended up with an over length add, that was bolded, appeared in 3 different sections, and lasted for 3 editions.

Then in 1998 I came across this little place on the internet called eBay. That's when my life changed. When I first started selling on ebay I was working off my kitchen table. Using eBay I was able to sell a lot more items a lot faster than I ever could at any garage sale. Using a manual cut and paste system I would list about 100 items at a time, which was a lot more than most sellers. Even though I was selling a lot I was still buying more than I was actually selling so I needed to do something and that's when I came across the idea of buying a house, not to live in but to use as storage for all the merchandise that I had for sale. Around this time I realized I needed some help and took the plunge into getting an employee. I also was able to pick up another small house next door to my storage house. I gave my employee free rent in exchange for him helping with the eBay business. He would package and inventory items for me. That worked out very well.

I kept growing and expanding and eventually bought a small warehouse. We moved into that warehouse and continued selling. Eventually I got a second employee and together they did most of the physical work for me, allowing me to concentrate on the computer side. However things still kept expanding and I needed to upscale again. I ended up buying a much larger warehouse. Around this time I had about 2500 items listed on eBay at any particular time.

Eventually I took in a partner. I met Jon at a real estate seminar I attended; he waited over 15 minutes just to talk to me. He had read some of the articles I had written for a friend's newsletter. We hit it off great and he easily passed a few tests I gave him. Over the next couple of years I trained him and told him all my secrets about how to do eBay efficiently and how to buy and sell merchandise on the secondary merchandise market. He became so good at it that I ended up consigning all of my merchandise to him and stopped selling myself. That worked out great. I could go out and buy stuff and not have to worry about selling it. I would just give it to my partner and have him do everything else that needed to be done and he just gave me a check at the end of each month. At this time we had increased the average number of eBay listings to about 5,000.

Eventually I realized there was another step, and that was consignment selling. Rather than buying product myself I would get the product from somebody else on consignment. That way I would not have to pay any cash to purchase the product. This allowed us to again increase our number of online auctions to about 10,000.

Eventually I turned the whole eBay business over to my partner and concentrated on other business ventures. As part of our expansion, we started up a live auction company called Buckaru Auctions. We currently run live and webcast auctions on a weekly basis.

Over the years I have seen a lot of people taken advantage of by unscrupulous companies claiming they can make people rich through eBay auctions and selling online. All they were doing was taking people's money and selling them premade online store fronts and telling them they can also sell on eBay. They promoted the classic drop shipping scam, which I devoted a full chapter on in this book. Because I did not want to see any more people taken advantage of I decided to start teaching people my principles and techniques about online auctions. This led to the development of an entire educational course package about eBay and selling by using online auctions.

Free Bonuses

How to Use eBay for Big Profit$:   a value of $49.99
A free Mp3 audio download with over 60 minutes on why eBay is the optimum business structure to maximize your profits.
Visit www.FastTrackToEbay.com/book

Buy Local and Sell Global: a value of $49.99
A free Mp3 Audio download that teaches you how to source product locally and sell it internationally for massive profits.
Visit www.FastTrackToEbay.com/book

EBay in Canada: a value of $49.99
A free Mp3 Audio download discussing specifics about using eBay in Canada and selling to the USA and the differences between USA and Canada.
Visit www.FastTrackToEbay.com/book

A Millionaire's Mindset: a value of $49.99
A free Mp3 Audio download giving you Insight into the mindset of a millionaire where you will learn a bit about business, real estate and the stock market.
Visit www.FastTrackToEbay.com/book

Fee Credit on Major Auction Site: a value of $49.99
When you register on this major Internet auction site, you will get a fee credit that you can use for various listing upgrades or on site advertising.
Visit www.FastTrackToEbay.com/book

Educational Grants and Credits: a value up to $3,499.99

We have a special Educational Grant program which helps students with the purchase of Advanced Educational materials. Also any purchase of our related advanced educational programs or products, will result in the same amount returned as a fee credit on a major internet auction site that you can use for various listing upgrades or on site advertising.
Visit www.FastTrackToEbay.com/book

www.ingramcontent.com/pod-product-compliance
Lightning Source LLC
Chambersburg PA
CBHW060040210326
41520CB00009B/1199